CHRISTMAS JOKES for KIDS

David MacLennan

FOLK LORE PUBLISHING

The Publisher: Folklore Publishing
Website: www.folklorepublishing.com

Library and Archives Canada Cataloguing in Publication

MacLennan, David, 1977–, author
    Christmas jokes for kids / David MacLennan.

ISBN 978-1-926677-91-0 (pbk.)

    1. Christmas—Humor—Juvenile literature. 2. Wit and humor, Juvenile.
I. Title.

PN6231.C36M33 2013   j394.266302'07   C2013-904873-1

Project Director: Faye Boer
Illustrations: Peter Tyler, Roger Garcia
Cover Images: Santa, elf & reindeer © HitToon.com / Shutterstock; Christmas
tree © Lorelyn Medina / Shutterstock; snow in foreground © colematt /
Photos.com

Produced with the assistance of the Government of
Alberta, Alberta Multimedia Development Fund.

We acknowledge the financial support of the Government of Canada
through the Canada Book Fund (CBF) for our publishing activities.

 Canadian   Patrimoine
Heritage   canadien

PC: 24

Contents

Introduction

Christmas is a time to be with family and friends to celebrate life, and a major part of life is laughter. Christmastime for my family was always a laugh riot. We are like any other family on Christmas Day—we wake up way too early, open presents, whip up a storm of wrapping paper and then settle down to enjoy our new gifts. But after we get bored with our presents, we all gather in the living room to sit and talk. But this is no ordinary What-did-you-get-this-year? chat. My family loves to tell jokes and funny stories. We sit around the fireplace for hours on Christmas Day and compete to see who can tell the funniest joke and make us laugh the loudest.

When I was younger, it was always my dad who was the funniest, often acting out most of his jokes. And he also made us laugh by pulling out his false teeth and making silly, stupid faces. I watched him closely and listened to him carefully and began keeping a record of the jokes he most liked to tell.

In this book you will find some of the stories and jokes that my family told during the holiday season, and I have added a few Christmas facts and quizzes so that you and your family can share in the fun. So instead of just opening presents and then disappearing into your room to play with that new video game, try getting everyone together to enjoy a little holiday laughter.

I guarantee that the adults in the room will need a good laugh once they see their credit card bills when Christmas is over.

CHAPTER ONE

The Naughty Kids

Christmas has been cancelled! And it's all your fault. You told Santa you had been good this year, and he died of laughter.

The Bad Sister

Sarah and her 13-year-old sister are fighting a lot. This happens when you combine a headstrong five-year-old, who is sure she is always right, with a young adolescent.

Sarah's parents, trying to take advantage of their young daughter's newfound interest in Santa Claus, remind her that Santa is watching and that he doesn't like it when children fight. This doesn't seem to change Sarah's behavior.

"I'll just have to call Santa and tell him about your misbehavior," Sarah's mother says as she picks up the phone and dials. Sarah's eyes grow big as her mother asks Mrs. Claus (who is really Sarah's aunt; Santa's real telephone line is busy) if she could put Santa on the phone. Sarah's mouth drops open in surprise when her mom talks to Santa

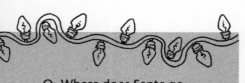

Q: Where does Santa go swimming?
A: At the North Pool.

(Sarah's uncle) and describes how Sarah has been acting. Then, Sarah's mom tells her daughter that Santa wants to talk to her, so Sarah reluctantly takes the phone.

Santa, in a deep voice, explains to Sarah that there will be no presents Christmas morning for children who fight with their sisters. He will be watching, and he expects things to be better from now on.

Q: What do reindeer hang on their Christmas trees?
A: Horn-aments.

Sarah, now even more wide-eyed, solemnly nods to each of Santa's remarks and then silently hangs up the phone when he is done.

After a few seconds, Sarah's mom (holding in her laughter at being so clever) asks, "What did Santa say to you, dear?"

In almost a whisper, Sarah sadly replies, "Santa said he won't be bringing toys to my sister this year."

At Gramma's

Two brothers are spending the night at their grandparents' home. At bedtime, the boys kneel beside their bed to say their prayers when the youngest one begins to pray at the top of his lungs:

"I pray for a new bicycle! I pray for a new Xbox! I pray for a new iPad!"

His older brother leans over, nudges his brother with his elbow and says, "Why are you shouting your prayers? God isn't deaf, ya know."

To which the little brother replies, "No, but Gramma is!"

Leroy's Letter

Little Leroy goes up to his mother and demands a new bicycle for Christmas. His mother decides that he should take a look at himself and the way he has been acting. She says, "Well, Leroy, it's almost Christmas, and we don't have the money to buy you anything you want. So why don't you write a letter to Jesus and pray for a bike."

Q: What does Scrooge wear to play ice hockey?

A: Cheap skates.

After Leroy has a temper tantrum, his mother sends him to his room. He finally sits down and writes a letter to Jesus.

Dear Jesus,
I've been a good boy this year and would appreciate a new bicycle.
Your Friend,
Leroy

Now, Leroy knows that Jesus sees what kind of boy he is (a brat), so he rips up the letter and decides to give it another try.

Dear Jesus,
I've been an okay boy this year, and I want a new bicycle.
Yours Truly,
Leroy

Well, Leroy knows he hasn't been totally honest, so he tears up the letter and tries again.

Dear Jesus,

I've thought about being a good boy this year, and can I have a bicycle?

Leroy

This time, Leroy looks deep down in his heart, which was what his mother really wanted in the first place. He knows he has been behaving terrible and deserves almost nothing. He crumples up the letter, throws it in the trashcan and runs outside. He walks around and is sad because of the way he treats his parents. He really thinks about his

Q: What do you get when you cross Santa Claus with chowder?

A: A jolly old elf that stuffs your stockings and empties your fridge.

actions. He suddenly finds himself in front of a Catholic Church. Leroy goes inside and kneels down. He looks around, not knowing what he should do. Leroy finally gets up and starts to walk out of the church when he sees all the statues. All of a sudden, he grabs a small one and runs out the door. He goes home, runs into his room and hides the statue under his bed and then writes this letter:

Jesus,

I've got your mama. If you ever want to see her again, give me a bike!

Sincerely,

You know who!

Free Ride

It is the day after Christmas in San Francisco, and Pastor Michael is looking at the nativity scene outside the church when he notices that baby Jesus is missing from the figures.

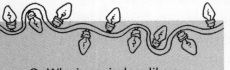

Q: Why is a reindeer like a gossip?

A: Because they are both tail bearers.

He immediately runs into his church office so he can call the police. As he is about to lift up the phone, he sees little Jimmy through the window with a red wagon, and in the wagon is the figure of the baby Jesus.

Pastor Michael walks up to Jimmy and says, "Well, Jimmy, where did you get the little infant?"

Jimmy replies, "I got him from the church."

"And why did you take him?"

With a sheepish smile, Jimmy replies, "Well, about a week before Christmas, I prayed to little Lord Jesus. I told him if he brought me a red wagon for Christmas, I would give him a ride around the block in it."

The Law and Kids

A police officer on a horse sees a young boy riding on the road and says to the kid, "Nice bike you got there. Did Santa bring that to you last Christmas?"

The kid says, "Yeah."

The cop says, "Well, next year, tell Santa to put a tail-light on that bike."

The cop then writes the kid a $20 ticket for violating bicycle safety.

The kid takes the ticket, and before he rides off, he says, "By the way, that's a nice horse you got there. Did Santa bring that to you?"

The cop decides to play along and says, "Yeah, he sure did."

The kid says, "Well, next year, tell Santa to put the stupidity in the horse's brain instead of on his back."

How Old Is Santa?

Suzie: "If Santa doesn't have to age, then how come he's so old?"

Jackie: "He only looks like he's old. He's really an undercover kid."

Curious Kid

A 10-year-old girl has been learning a lot about the Bible from her grandmother and is becoming quite knowledgeable about the events described in the Bible. One day while visiting her grandmother, the girl shocks her grandmother by asking, "Which virgin was the

Q: What do reindeer have that no other animals have?

A: Baby reindeer.

mother of Jesus? The Virgin Mary or the King James Virgin?"

Shopping for Gifts

It is early November, and a man is brought before a judge. The judge asks the man, "What are you charged with?"

"Doing my Christmas shopping early," replies the young man.

"That's not an offense," says the judge. "How early were you doing this shopping?"

"Before the store opened," replies the man.

Visiting Santa

A little girl goes to visit Santa with her mom at a busy mall in Toronto. After waiting in line with all the other kids for a long time, the girl finally gets to climb onto Santa's lap, smiling from ear to ear.

Santa asks the girl the usual question: "And what would you like for Christmas this year?"

The girl stares at him with her mouth wide open. She is horrified for a minute, then gasps, "What! Didn't you get my email?!"

Q: Why do reindeer wear black boots?

A: Because their brown ones are all muddy.

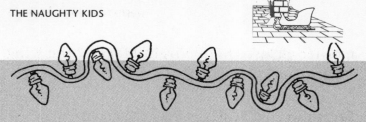

Signs That Santa Is Starting to Hate Kids

8. Your letter to the North Pole comes back stamped, "Dream on, Chester!"

7. You ask for a new bike and instead get a snow shovel.

6. Along with presents, Santa leaves you a big bill for shipping and handling.

5. By the time Santa gets to your house, all he has left is foam packing.

4. On Christmas Day, you wake up with a reindeer head in your bed.

3. Instead of "Naughty" or "Nice," Santa has put you on the "Stupid" list.

2. The labels on all your toys read "Straight from Craptown."

1. You go to visit Santa and he says, "Off my lap, Tubby!"

Note Left for Santa

Dear Santa,
If you leave me a new bike under our Christmas tree, I will give you the antidote to the poison I put in the milk.
Love,
Timmy

A Test at Christmas

Tommy's house is packed with relatives for Christmas dinner. Tommy's grandpa asks his six-year-old grandson about school, his friends and what he does for fun. After a while, Grandpa notices that Tommy is losing interest in the conversation so he pulls out two bills from his wallet—$10 and $20. He shows both bills to Tommy and tells him that he can keep any bill he chooses.

Q: What does Scrooge do when it's cold outside?

A: Sits by a candle.

Tommy reaches over and grabs the $10. Grandpa is pretty surprised and upset about the unwise decision his grandson has made, so he pulls out another $10 to see if Tommy has just made a mistake. Again, Grandpa tells Tommy to take one of the bills and keep it.

Tommy grabs the other $10. Grandpa again is surprised and upset. He takes Tommy over to one of the uncles and tells him how dumb Tommy is for choosing the $10 over the $20.

Grandpa goes around the living room to every uncle, aunt and cousin to show them that Tommy chooses the $10 over the $20. Grandpa finally shows the stunt to Tommy's dad. The dad is quite surprised but doesn't pay too much attention because he is busy talking to his guests.

A few hours later, the dad thinks about Tommy's poor decision and is worried about his son and his math skills. He asks his son if he knows the difference between $10 and $20.

"Of course," replies Tommy.

"So why did you always choose the $10 over the $20?" asks the dad.

Tommy, with a big smile, says, "Well, Dad, if I would have chosen the first $20, do you think Grandpa would have played the game 12 more times?"

Dumb Crook

It's Christmas Eve, and a department store manager is in his office paying the hired Santa. All of a sudden, a teenager carrying a gun bursts into the room and orders the manager to hand over all the money.

The manager is wondering what to do, so the teenager fires his gun in the air to force the manager to make up his mind. The frightened manager quickly opens the till and hands

Q: What does Scrooge do when it's really cold outside?
A: He lights the candle.

over the money. The robber pulls the trigger again, but nothing happens, so, unbelievably, the teenager peers down the barrel and then fires again.

This time it works.

A Test to See if You're a Grinch

Grab a pencil and a piece of paper and mark down your points.

1. You reuse last year's Christmas cards and send them out under your own name. (5 points)

2. You sneak a look at your presents and then complain about what you're getting. (5 points)

3. You have dressed your dog or cat as Santa Claus, elf helper or reindeer. (10 points for each animal. If you dressed up your pet as an endangered species, add 5 extra points.)

4. You put out last year's stale cookies and a glass of sour buttermilk for Santa. (1 point for each stale cookie. If you leave Santa a fruitcake, add 20 points.)

5. You enclose a cheap gift from Target, Walmart or the Dollar Store in a box from Bloomingdale's, or another expensive store, to impress your friends. (5 points for each gift)

6. You make long-distance phone calls to your friends on Christmas Day claiming you are stuck in a phone booth. (5 points; 10 if you call from your mom's cellphone)

7. During your school Christmas party, you stuff huge piles of cookies in your pocket to eat at

A Test to See if You're a Grinch, continued

home later. (5 points; 15 points if you serve the cookies at your own Christmas party at home)

8. At your friend's Christmas party, you bring a store-bought fruitcake and say your mom made it. (5 points; 15 points if the fruitcake is from last year)

9. You steal toys from the Toys R Us collection bins for the poor, needy kids. (20 points)

Now add up your score on the "Grinch Scale":

20–30 points: You're a cheeseball.

31–50 points: You're training to be a Christmas thief and are probably wanted by the police.

51–100: Grinch, move over; you have serious competition!

Doh!

Jessica, who is seven, is opening her presents on Christmas morning. All of a sudden she stops, looks at her father with a tear in her eye and says,

Q: How do you make a slow reindeer fast?
A: Don't feed it.

"Wow, I must have been a bad girl this year."

"Why do you say that?" asks the father.

"Because I got a lot of clothes!"

Hello?

One day, the phone rings at Little Johnny's home, and he answers it.

Caller: "May I speak to your parents?"

Little Johnny: "They're busy."

Caller: "Oh. Is anybody else there?"

Little Johnny: "The police."

Caller: "Can I speak to them?"

Little Johnny: "They're busy."

Caller: "Oh. Is anybody else there?"

Little Johnny: "The firemen."

Caller: "Can I speak to them?"

Little Johnny: "They're busy."

Caller: "So let me get this straight—your parents, the police and the firemen are there, but they're all busy? It's Christmas, so what are they doing all in one place?"

Little Johnny: "Looking for me."

The Long List

Mark visits Santa in a department store, and the young boy has a long list of requests. Mark starts to read out his list to Santa: a bicycle, a sled, a chemistry set, a cowboy suit, a set of trains, a baseball glove and a skateboard.

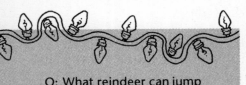

Q: What reindeer can jump higher than a house?

A: They all can! Houses can't jump!

"That's a pretty long list," Santa says sternly. "I'll have to check my book to see if you were a good boy this year."

"No, no," Marks says quickly and jumps off Santa's lap. "Never mind checking. I'll just take the skateboard."

Lost Purse

A woman loses her handbag while doing some Christmas shopping at Toys R Us. An honest little boy finds the purse and returns it to her.

Q: Who was Ebenezer Scrooge?

A: The Wizard of Bahs.

Looking in her purse, the woman says, "Hmmm...That's strange. When I lost my purse, there was one $100 bill in it. Now there are five $20 bills."

The boy quickly replies, "That's right, lady. The last time I found a lady's purse, she didn't have any change for a reward."

A Poor, Poor, Poor Kid Story

Last week I was rushing around at the mall trying to get some last-minute Christmas shopping done. I was stressed out and not thinking fondly of the season right then. It was dark, cold and wet in the parking lot as I started loading my car up with gifts. I noticed that I was missing a receipt that I might need later. So, mumbling under my breath, I started to walk back to the mall entrance. As I was searching the wet pavement for the lost receipt, I heard a quiet sobbing. The crying was coming from a poorly dressed boy of about 12 years old. He was short and thin. He was wearing only a ragged flannel shirt to protect him from the cold night's chill. Oddly enough, he was holding a $100 bill in his hand.

Thinking that the boy had lost his parents, I asked him what was wrong. He told me his sad story. He said he had three brothers and four sisters. His father had died when he was nine years old. His mother worked two full-time jobs. However, she had managed to save $200 to buy her children Christmas presents. The young boy said his mom dropped him off at the mall on the way to her second job. He was to use the $200 to buy presents for all his siblings and save just enough to take the bus home. As he was walking to the mall door, an older boy grabbed one of the $100 out of his hand and ran away.

Q: Why don't Prancer and Dancer and the other reindeer overtake Rudolph?

A: Because they don't believe in passing the buck.

"Why didn't you scream for help?" I asked.

The boy said, "I did!"

"And nobody came to help you?"

The boy stared at the sidewalk and sadly shook his head.

"How loud did you scream?" I asked.

The soft-spoken boy looked up and meekly whispered, "Help me."

Q: What's the difference between a reindeer and a snowball?

A: They're both brown, except the snowball.

I realized that absolutely no one could hear that poor boy cry for help. So I grabbed his other $100 and ran.

Dating

On Christmas Eve, a teenage girl brings her new boyfriend home to meet her parents, who are shocked by the boy's appearance: black leather jacket, motorcycle boots, tattoos and a pierced nose.

Later, the parents pull their daughter aside and express their concern.

"Dear," says the mother in a soft voice, "he doesn't seem very nice."

"Oh, please, Mom," replies the daughter, "if he wasn't nice, why would he be doing 100 hours of community service!"

Q: What does Santa call that three-legged reindeer?

A: Eileen.

How to Make Santa Angry

1. Leave him a note, explaining that you've gone away for the holidays. Ask if he would mind cleaning your room.

2. Keep an angry bull in your living room. If you think a bull goes crazy when he sees a little red cape, wait until he sees that big, red Santa suit!

3. Build an army of snowmen on the roof that are holding these signs: "Bah Humbug" and "Bite me, Santa."

4. When Santa comes down the chimney, call the police and charge Santa with break-and-enter.

5. While Santa is in your house, find his sleigh and sit in it. As soon as he comes back and sees you, tell him that he shouldn't have missed that last payment and then take off.

7. Leave out a copy of your Christmas list with last-minute changes and corrections.

8. While Santa is in your house, cover the top of the chimney with barbed wire.

9. Dress up like the Easter Bunny. Wait for Santa to come down the chimney and then say, "This neighborhood ain't big enough for the both of us."

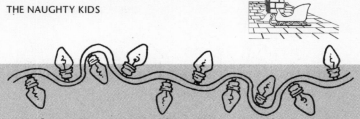

Other Ways to Make Santa Really Angry

1. Instead of leaving Santa milk and cookies, leave him a salad and a note saying that you think he could lose a few pounds.

2. While he's in your house, go find his sleigh and write him a speeding ticket.

3. Replace all his reindeer with exact replicas. Then wait and see what happens when he tries to get them to fly.

4. Leave a note by the telephone telling Santa that Mrs. Claus called and wants him to pick up some milk and a loaf of bread on his way home.

5. Leave out a plate filled with cookies and a glass of milk with a note that says, "For the Tooth Fairy. :)" Leave another plate out with half a stale cookie and a few drops of skim milk in a dirty glass with a note that says, "For Santa. :("

6. Leave Santa a note saying that you've moved. Include a map with unclear and hard-to-read directions to your new house.

7. Paint "hoof-prints" all over your face and clothes. While Santa is in your house, go out on the roof. When he goes back to the roof, act like you've been "trampled" by his reindeer. Threaten to take him to court.

Christmas for Osama

Little David comes home from first grade and tells his father that the class learned about the history of Christmas Day. "Since Christmas is for the Christians, and we're Jewish," David says, "will God get mad at me for giving someone a Christmas present?"

David's father thinks for a moment, then says, "No, I don't think God would get mad. Who do you want to give a present to?"

"Osama Bin Laden," David says.

"Why Osama Bin Laden?" his father asks in shock.

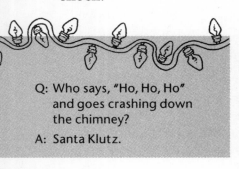

Q: Who says, "Ho, Ho, Ho" and goes crashing down the chimney?

A: Santa Klutz.

"Well," David says, "I thought that if a little American Jewish boy could have enough love to give Osama a Christmas present, God might start to think that maybe we're not all bad, and if other kids saw what I did and sent presents to Osama, too, God would love everyone a lot more. And then God would travel all over the world to tell everyone how much he loved them."

The father's heart swells, and he looks at his son with pride. "David, that's the most wonderful thing I've ever heard."

"I know," David says, "and once that gets Osama out in the open, the Marines can shoot him."

Tasty Gift

Four-year-old Randy loves candy almost as much as his mom does. So for Christmas, Randy and his daddy give her a huge box of choco-

Q: What do reindeer say before telling you a joke?

A: This one will sleigh you.

lates. A few days later, Randy is eyeing the candy in the box, wishing to have a piece of it.

As he reaches out to touch one of the bigger pieces of chocolate, his mom says to him, "Now, Randy. You know that if you touch one piece, then you have to eat it. Do you understand?"

"Oh, yes," Randy says, nodding his head and wiping his runny nose with his hand. Suddenly his little hand pats the tops of all the chocolates and he says, "Now I have to eat them all."

CHAPTER TWO

Santa, Mrs. Claus and the Reindeer

Santa Claus has the right idea. Visit people once a year.

Pay Here

First girl: "You don't see many reindeer in zoos, do you?"

Second girl: "No. They can't afford the admission."

Truth About Reindeer

According to the Alaska Department of Fish and Game, although both male and female reindeer grow antlers in the summer each year, male reindeer drop their antlers at the beginning of winter, usually from late November to mid-December. Female reindeer keep their antlers until after they give birth in the spring.

Q: How do you get four polar bears in a car?

A: Take the reindeer out first.

Therefore—despite every story that says Santa's reindeer, every one of them, from Rudolph to

Blitzen were boys—the reindeer were girls.

We should've known that only women would be able to drag a fat man in a red velvet suit all around the world in one night and not get lost.

Q: What game do reindeer play in their stalls?

A: Stable tennis.

Noisy

Santa Claus: "What's that terrible racket outside?"

Mrs. Claus: "It's rain, deer."

Sleigh Problems

Santa's sleigh breaks down on Christmas Eve. He flags down a passing motorist and asks, "Can you give me a hand? My sleigh broke down, and I need some help, please."

"Sorry," the driver replies. "I wish I could help you, but I'm not a mechanic. I'm a foot doctor."

"Well, can you give me a toe?"

How Many Reindeer?

Did you know that according to the song, "Rudolph, the Red-nosed Reindeer," Santa has 12 reindeer? Sure, just look at the words:

"There's Dasher and Dancer and Prancer and Vixen, Comet and Cupid and Donner and Blitzen..." That makes eight reindeer.

Then there's Rudolph, of course, so that makes nine.

Then there's Olive. You know, "Olive the other reindeer used to laugh..." That makes 10.

The eleventh reindeer is Howe. You know, "Then Howe the reindeer loved him..." Eleven reindeer.

Oh, and the twelfth reindeer? That's Andy! "Andy shouted out with glee."

The proof is in the song!

Dad Knows Best

Father to his three-year-old son: "No, Billy, a reindeer is not a horse with a TV antenna on his head."

Strong Kid

First boy: "I'm so strong I could lift a reindeer with one hand!"

Second boy: "Yeah, but where are you going to find a one-handed reindeer?"

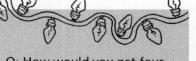

Q: How would you get four reindeer in a car?

A: Two in the front and two in the back.

Reindeer Names

First elf: "Santa Claus has two reindeer. He calls one Edward and

the other one Edward! I bet you can't tell me why he does that!"

Second elf: "Oh, yes I can. Because two Eds are better than one, of course!"

Q: What do you call the reindeer with cotton wool in his ears?

A: You can call him anything you want to—he won't hear you.

Is That You?

After Christmas, Santa Claus decides he needs a vacation. He goes to Texas because it is warm, and he has heard that the people are friendly.

As soon as he arrives in Austin, people begin to point and say, "Look! The big red one! Isn't he someone famous?"

Santa thinks to himself, "Gee, I'll never get any rest if people start asking to sit on my lap and try to tell me what they want for Christmas next year." So he decides to disguise himself. He buys a cowboy outfit complete with cowboy boots and a cowboy hat. "No one will know me now. I look just like everyone else!" he thinks happily.

As soon as Santa starts walking down the street, people begin to point and say, "Look! It's that famous Christmas personality!"

Santa quickly runs around a corner to hide. "It's my beard!" he says to himself. "They recognize me because of my long white beard!" So Santa goes to a barbershop and has his beard shaved off. "I really look like everybody else now!" Santa thinks. So he walks down the street with a big smile on his face.

Suddenly a man shouts, "It's him! It's him! Look, everybody!"

Santa can't believe it. He is sure that no one would recognize him. So Santa walks up to the man and says, "How did you recognize me?"

The man looks at Santa and says, "You? I don't know you—but isn't that four-legged guy behind you with the big red nose, Rudolph?"

A Funny Boy

First boy: "What has antlers, pulls Santa's sleigh and is made of cement?"

Second boy: "I don't know."

First boy: "A reindeer!"

Second boy: "What about the cement?"

First boy: "I just threw that in to make it hard."

Time for a Change

Christmas is over. Santa and his reindeer finally have a chance to rest after all their hard work. And they deserve it. They have done a good job of delivering presents to all the girls and boys.

Q: Why did the reindeer wear sunglasses at the beach?

A: Because he didn't want to be recognized.

Rudolph now has a chance to do something he has wanted to do for a long time. He makes an appointment with a plastic surgeon because he is so sensitive about his looks.

However, it isn't his glowing nose that he wants to change. He is proud of his nose and the help he has given Santa because of it. No, he is sensitive about his

Q: What do you call a black-and-blue reindeer?

A: Bruce.

long ears, which are much more prominent than the ears of the average reindeer, or a bear for that matter.

So one week after Christmas, Rudolph lets the doctor do the surgery, and since that time, January 1 has been celebrated as...New Ears Day.

Reindeer Pun

It is the night before Christmas, and Santa Claus' sleigh team is one reindeer short because Prancer suddenly becomes ill.

When an inflatable plastic reindeer is used to take Prancer's place, so that no one will notice the missing reindeer, the Chief of Elves asks Santa, "Is that your vinyl Prancer?"

Visiting Santa

A list of comments kids have made to Santa at the mall:

- "Santa, when you come down the chimney this year, watch out for the fire."

- "I don't feel so well...Barfffff!"

- "I want two fire trucks. One for me, and one for the poor kids."

- "All I want for Christmas is to stop peeing every time I sit on somebody's lap."

- "Daddy said to ask if you could help improve his golf game."

- "Your breath smells."

- "When you were a kid, who brought you presents?"

- "If girls have cooties, do they get gifts?"

- "Don't give anything to my brother. He pees his bed."

- "What I want for Christmas is for you to take away these head lice."

- "If my sister tells you what I did, she's lying."

Letter from Santa Claus

To: All Residents in the Southern United States

Re: Replacement Santa

I'm sorry to tell you that effective immediately, I will no longer be able to fly to the Southern United States on Christmas Eve. Because the population of the earth is getting so large, I can only fly to certain areas of Ohio, Indiana, Illinois, Wisconsin and Michigan.

As part of my new and better contract, I will also get longer breaks for milk and cookies, so keep that in mind, kids! (More cookies! And sometimes you can leave out a chocolate cake, too!)

Q: What's the name of the reindeer with three humps on its back?

A: Humphrey.

However, I'm certain that children will be in good hands with my replacement who happens to be my third cousin, Bubba Claus. His side of the family is from the South Pole.

Bubba shares my goal of delivering toys to all the good boys and girls; however, there are a few differences between us:

1. There is no danger of a Grinch stealing your presents from Bubba Claus. He has a gun rack on his sleigh and a bumper sticker that reads "These toys insured by Smith and Wesson."

2. Instead of milk and cookies, Bubba Claus prefers that children leave a RC Cola and pork rinds

(or a moon pie) on the fireplace. And Bubba doesn't smoke a pipe. He dips a little snuff though, so please have an empty spit can handy.

3. Bubba Claus' sleigh is pulled by floppy-eared, flyin' dogs instead of reindeer. I made the mistake of loaning Bubba a reindeer one time, and Blitzen's head is now over Bubba's fireplace.

4. You won't hear "On Comet, on Cupid, on Donner and Blitzen" when Bubba Claus arrives. Instead you'll hear, "On Earnhardt, on Wallace, on Martin and LaBonte. On Rudd, on Jarrett, on Elliot and Petty."

5. "Ho, ho, ho!" has been replaced by "Yee haw!" And you are likely to also hear Bubba's elves reply, "I her'd dat!"

6. As required by the highway laws in the southern U.S., Bubba Claus' sleigh will have a Yosemite Sam safety triangle on the back with the words, "Back Off!" The last I heard, Bubba's sleigh has other decorations on the back as well—one is a drawing of me (Santa Claus) peeing on the Tooth Fairy.

7. The usual Christmas movie classics such as *Miracle on 34th Street* and *It's a Wonderful Life* will not be shown in your viewing area. Instead, you will see the movie *Home Alone* and *Silent Night, Deadly Night*, an awful horror movie about a killer Santa. (Don't worry, kids—it's

Q: What does Santa call that reindeer with no eyes?

A: No-eye-deer.

just a movie. I am a good Santa. But there is that other Claus cousin of mine that we don't speak about anymore.)

Q: What do you call a reindeer with only one eye that has no legs?

A: Still no-eye-deer.

8. And finally, Bubba Claus doesn't wear a belt. If I were you, I'd make sure your family turns the other way when he bends over to put presents under the tree.

Sincerely,

Santa Claus

Letter to Santa

Dear Santa,

My mom told me to write to you and to say thanks for the train set. My dad plays with it all the time. Can you send me another one?

John

Weather in Russia

A long time ago, in Russia, there was a famous weather man named Rudolf. He's always had a 100-percent accuracy rate for his forecasts of the Russian weather conditions. He was really good at predicting when it would rain.

One night, despite clear skies, he makes the prediction on the evening news that a violent storm is approaching. It will flood the town in which he and his wife live. Rudolf warns the people to take proper precautions and prepare for the worst.

Q: Why are Santa's reindeer like a horse race?
A: Because they both get stopped by the rein.

After he arrives home later that evening, his wife meets him at the door and starts arguing with him, telling him that his weather prediction is the most ridiculous thing she has ever heard. This time, she says, he has made a terrible mistake. There isn't a cloud anywhere within 10 miles of the village, she tells him. As a matter of fact, the day has been the most beautiful day that the town has ever seen, and it is quite obvious that it simply *wasn't going to rain.*

Rudolf tells his wife to be quiet and to listen to him. If he says it's going to rain, it will rain! He has all of his Russian heritage behind him, he tells his wife, and he knows what he's talking about. His wife argues that although he comes from a proud heritage, *it still isn't going to rain.*

The couple argue so much so that they go to bed angry at each other.

During the night, sure enough, one of the worst rainstorms hits the village. The next morning, when Rudolf and his wife get out of bed, they look out the window and see all the rain that had fallen during the night.

"See," says Rudolf, "I told you it was going to rain!"

His wife says, "Once again, your prediction has come true. But I want to know something...how were you able to be so accurate, Rudolf?"

He replies, "You see, Rudolf the Red knows rain, dear!"

I Think Santa Claus Is My Mom

I hate to take away this myth, but I believe Santa is my mom. Think about it. Christmas is a big, organized, warm, fuzzy, happy day, and I have a tough time believing a dad could possibly do all that stuff, and here's why:

- Most dads don't even think about buying gifts until Christmas Eve at four o'clock. That's the time when they phone other forgetful dads and plan for a last-minute shopping spree. Once at the mall, dads always seem surprised to find only As Seen on TV products, socket wrench sets

  Knock, knock!
  Who's there?
  Pudding!
  Pudding who?
  Pudding in your face!

  and tech gadgets left on the shelves. (You might think this would make the dads panic, but my dad tells me it's an enormous relief because he doesn't have to decide what to buy.) Therefore, I'm convinced Santa is my Mom.

- If Santa was my dad, everyone in the universe would wake up on Christmas morning to find

a rotating musical Chia Pet under the tree, still in the shopping bag.

• Even if my dad was Santa and *did* have reindeer, he'd still have problems because he would get lost up there in the snow and clouds and refuse to stop and ask for directions.

• There would also be delays in the chimney, where the Mike Holmes–like Santa would stop to inspect and fix the bricks. He would also check for carbon monoxide fumes in every gas fireplace and get under every Christmas tree that is crooked to straighten it to a perfectly upright 90° angle.

• Other reasons why Santa is probably my mom:
  → My dad can't pack a bag.
  → My dad would rather be dead than be caught wearing red velvet.
  → My dad would refuse to allow his body to be described as a "bowlful of jelly."

Mrs. Claus Cooking

Santa Claus is on his way home after Christmas and decides to stop at a hotel to rest for the night. When he wakes up the next morning, he is hungry and calls room service. "I want a breakfast of two eggs burned black around the edges, undercooked

bacon, weak coffee, watery orange juice and cold, hard, unbuttered toast," orders Santa.

"Why would you want a terrible breakfast like that?" asks the room service guy.

"I'm homesick," replies Santa.

First Dinner

Santa comes home after working hard on Christmas Eve to find his wife crying. "Darling, whatever is the matter?" he asks her.

"Sweetheart," Mrs. Claus sobs, "the most terrible thing has happened! I cooked my very first roast chicken for you, and when I took it out of the oven to season it, the phone rang. When I went back to the kitchen after hanging up the phone, I found that the cat had eaten the chicken!"

"Don't worry, darling," says Santa. "Don't cry. It'll be okay. We can get a new cat tomorrow."

Smart Answer

Young brother: "Is there really a Mrs. Santa Claus?"

Older brother: "The best way to know for sure is to ask Santa Claus the next time you see him."

Q: What do you call a reindeer wearing ear muffs?

A: Anything you want because he can't hear you!

Top 10 Reasons Santa Needs to Give Himself a Raise

10. The long hours, the bad weather and the smaller chimneys.

9. Nike won't give him a lucrative side-contract.

8. Reindeer and elves have unionized, driving up his cost.

7. There's a new tax on flying sleighs.

6. Insurance for flying a sleigh has tripled over the past two years.

5. He needs extra cash to cover his off-season gambling losses.

4. Air traffic controllers are demanding higher wages.

3. The cost of living has increased at the North Pole.

2. Children don't leave him as many cookies as they used to.

1. Mrs. Claus told him to.

CHAPTER THREE

The Elves, Snowmen, Animals and Life in the North

This holiday season, instead of gifts, I've decided to give everyone my opinion.

How Cold Is It?

"It's so cold outside," the elf says to Santa, "that I just saw a polar bear jump from one iceberg to another, and the bear froze in mid-air!"

"That's impossible," says Santa. "The law of gravity won't allow that!"

Q: What did the seal say when it swam into a concrete wall?

A: "Dam!"

"Oh, I know," replies the elf, "but the law of gravity is frozen, too!"

Good Noses

Two snowmen are in a field, and one turns to the other and says, "I don't know about you, but I can smell carrots!"

Hungry Polar Bears

During Christmas vacation, three boys decide to go visit an indoor zoo. A zookeeper approaches them while they are standing near the polar bear cage and asks them their names and what they're up to.

The first boy says, "My name's Tommy, and I was trying to feed peanuts to the polar bears."

The second boy says, "My name's Billy, and I was trying to feed peanuts to the polar bears."

The third boy says, "My name is Peanuts."

Snowstorm

On Christmas Eve during a violent snowstorm with howling winds and blowing snow in a small town in Alaska, a mother is tucking her young son into bed. The wind is shaking the windows, and the boy is afraid. The mom is about to turn off the light when the boy asks with a trembling voice, "Mommy, will you sleep with me tonight?"

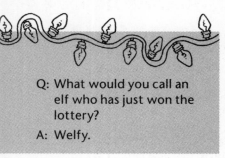

Q: What would you call an elf who has just won the lottery?

A: Welfy.

His mother smiles and gives him a hug. "I can't dear," she says. "You're a big boy now. I have to sleep in daddy's room."

After a long silence, the little boy says, "The big sissy."

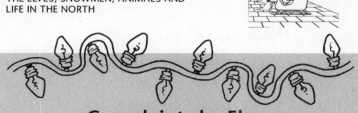

Complaints by Elves

- We work for 364 days a year just to make children smile, and no one cares. But if someone dances around one day in some stupid outfit in February with a lousy bow and arrow, all of a sudden he's a hero.

- The company health plan doesn't cover special shoes to make us look taller.

- The icy-cold North Pole temperature makes it hard for us to produce quality toys.

- We don't like reindeer game number 12: elf lacrosse.

- We're constantly ridiculed for that 0–854 score in the North Pole basketball league.

- Jolly Ole Santa never brings back a single cookie to share with us.

- Working for thousands of years and not once did an elf ever get a thank you letter from those greedy little kids.

- It's freezing cold up north!

Twelve Cat Days of Christmas

On the twelfth day of Christmas my human
gave to me,
Twelve bags of catnip,
Eleven tarter Pounce treats,
Ten ornaments hanging,
Nine wads of Kleenex,
Eight peacock feathers,
Seven stolen Q-tips,
Six feathered balls,
Five milk jug rings,
Four munchy house plants,
Three running faucets,
Two fuzzy mousies,
And a hamster in a plastic ball!

Walking in a Doggy Wonderland

Dog tags ring, are you listenin'?
In the lane, snow is glistenin'.
It's yellow, not white—I've been there tonight,
Marking up my winter wonderland.

Smell that tree? That's my fragrance.
It's a sign for wand'ring vagrants;
"Avoid where I pee, it's my pro-per-ty!
Marked up as my winter wonderland."

In the meadow Dad will build a snowman,
Following the classical design.
Then I'll lift my leg and let it go, man.
So all the world will know it's
Mine, mine, mine!

Straight from me to the fencepost,
Flows my natural incense boast;
"Stay off of my turf, this small piece of earth,
I mark it as my winter wonderland.

Fly!

Birdie, birdie in the sky,
Dropped some white stuff in my eye.
I'm a big girl, I won't cry,
Oh no! I forgot that reindeer can fly.

Singing Parrot

A few days before Christmas, a man goes into a pet store looking for a special gift for his wife. The store manager tells him he has just what he's looking for! A beautiful parrot named Chet that sings Christmas carols.

Q: What did the big furry hat say to the warm woolly scarf?

A: "You hang around while I go on ahead."

He brings the husband over to a colorful but quiet bird. The man agrees that Chet certainly is pretty, but he doesn't seem to be much for singing.

Q: Where does a snowman keep his money?

A: In a snowbank.

The manager tells him to watch as he reaches into his pocket and pulls out a lighter. The manager then clicks the lighter and holds it under Chet's left foot. Immediately, Chet starts singing the song "Silent Night, Holy Night."

The husband is very impressed with Chet's singing abilities and watches as the manager moves the lighter underneath Chet's right foot. Chet now starts to sing, "Jingle bells, jingle all the way." The husband says Chet is perfect and that he'll take him. The husband rushes home to his wife and insists upon giving her this wonderful gift immediately.

He presents Chet and starts to explain the parrot's special talent. Demonstrating, he holds a lighter under Chet's left foot and the bird sings "Silent Night." He then moves the lighter under the parrot's right foot, and Chet lets loose a round of "Jingle Bells." The wife is very impressed and asks her husband what happens if he holds the lighter between Chet's legs instead. Curious, the husband moves the lighter between the bird's legs, and the bird begins to sing "Chet's nuts roasting on an open fire!"

Dog Rules for Christmas

From one dog to another:

1. Be really patient with your humans during this holiday. They may appear to be more stressed-out than usual, and they will appreciate long, comforting dog cuddles.

2. They may come home with large bags of things they call "gifts." Do not assume that all the gifts are yours.

3. Be patient if your humans put decorations on you or make you wear silly clothes. They seem to get some special kind of pleasure out of seeing how you look with fake antlers.

4. They may bring a large tree into the house and cover it with lights and decorations. Bizarre as this may seem to you, it's an important ritual for your humans, so here are some things you need to know:

   • Don't pee on the tree.
   • Don't drink water in the container that holds the tree.
   • Be careful of your tail when you are near the tree.
   • If there are packages under the tree, even ones that smell interesting or have your name on them, don't rip them open.

Dog Rules for Christmas, continued

- And don't chew on the cord that runs from the funny-looking hole in the wall to the tree.

5. Your humans might invite a lot of strangers to come visit during the holidays. These parties can be fun, but they also call for good behavior on your part:
   - Not all strangers appreciate sloppy kisses with your tongue.
   - Don't eat off the buffet table. Beg for good-ies instead.
   - Be pleasant, even if the strangers sit on your spot on the sofa—they don't know any better.
   - Don't drink out of glasses that are left within your reach unless you can get away with it.

6. Your humans may also take you visiting. Your manners will be important:
   - Observe all the rules as stated in number 4 for trees that may be in other people's houses. (The first point is very important.)
   - Respect the territory of other animals that may live in the house. And yes, that includes the cat.
   - Be nice to the kiddies. They might feed you later.
   - Turn on your charm big time. Wag your tail a lot.

7. A fat man with a long white beard and a very loud laugh may emerge from your fireplace in the middle of the night. Do Not Bite Him!

The Football-playing Turkey

The pro football team has just finished their daily practice session when a large turkey comes strutting onto the field. While the players gaze in amazement, the turkey walks up to the head coach and demands a tryout.

Everyone stares in silence as the turkey catches pass after pass and runs right through the defensive line. When the turkey returns to the sidelines, the coach shouts, "You're terrific! Sign up for the season, and I'll see to it that you get a huge bonus."

"Forget the bonus," the turkey replies. "All I want to know is, does the season go past Christmas Day?"

Chatty

As an early Christmas present, a man gets a talking parrot from his friend. He takes the parrot home and puts it in his living room. But every time the man goes near the living

Q: Why do seals swim in salt water?

A: Because pepper water makes them sneeze.

room, he hears the parrot shouting insults at him. In desperation, he puts the parrot in the freezer to shut it up.

After a few minutes, the insults stop. Thinking he might have killed the parrot, the man takes it out of the freezer.

The parrot is still alive, but it is shivering. It stammers, "I'm s-sorry for b-b-being s-s-so rude. P-p-please f-f-forgive m-m-me."

So the man forgives him.

After a few seconds, the parrot asks, "So what exactly did the turkey do?"

Cards from Your Pets

From the Cats

We, your cats,
at Christmas say,
Thanks for caring
for us each day.
We love this season,
all green and red,
And by the way,
the hamster's dead.

From the Cat and Fish

Meow, glub, meow, glub,
a Merry Christmas wish.
Meow, glub, meow, glub,
from your cat and goldfish.

From the Pig

I've always loved the Christmas feast.
I've heard this year it's ham.
Too bad I've other plans this time.
Love, Your Pot-bellied Pig named Sam.

Worried About Santa

On Christmas morning, after a long night of delivering presents around the world, Rudolph is complaining to Prancer and Dancer. He says, "Santa got me the wrong present this year. I'm beginning to worry about the old man. I think he might be dyslexic."

Knock, knock!
Who's there?
Centipede!
Centipede who?
Centipede on the
Christmas tree!

"What makes you think that?" asks Dancer.

"Because he got me a Pony Sleigh Station!"

CHAPTER FOUR

Strange Christmas

Christmas is just plain weird. What other time of the year do you sit in front of a dead tree in your living room eating candy and snacks out of your socks?

Sheep!

One Christmas, Phil and Willy build a skating rink in the middle of a pasture and shoot the puck around for a few hours. When they are ready to head home, they see a shepherd leading his flock of sheep. The shepherd decides to take a shortcut across the rink. The sheep, however, are afraid of the ice and won't cross it. Desperate, the shepherd begins tugging the sheep to the other side.

Q: Why is a Christmas tree that has been chopped down called a "live Christmas tree"?

A: It's dead but doesn't know it, and yet it's having the time of its life.

"Look at that," says Phil to Willy. "That guy is trying to pull the wool over our ice!"

Christmas Weather Report

Turkeys will thaw in the morning, then warm in the oven to an afternoon high near 190°F. The kitchen will turn hot and humid, and if you bother the cook, be ready for a severe squall or cold shoulder.

During the late afternoon and evening, the cold front of a knife will slice through the turkey, causing an accumulation of one to two inches on plates. Mashed potatoes will drift across one side while cranberry sauce creates slippery spots on the other. Please pass the gravy.

Knock, knock!
Who's there?
Hanna!
Hanna who?
Hanna partridge in a pear tree!

A weight watch and indigestion warning have been issued for the entire area, with increased stuffiness around the beltway. During the evening, the turkey will diminish and taper off to leftovers, dropping to a low of 34°F in the refrigerator.

Looking ahead to the next two days, high pressure to eat sandwiches will be established. Flurries of leftovers can be expected both days with a 50-percent chance of scattered soup late in the day. We expect a warming trend where soup develops.

By early next week, eating pressure will be low as the only wish left will be the bone.

Santa Claus Is Tapping Your Cellphone

You better watch out,
You better not cry,
You better not pout,
I'm telling you why,
Santa Claus is tapping
Your phone.
He's bugging your room,
He's reading your email,
He's keeping a file
And running a tail.
Santa Claus is tapping
Your phone.
So you mustn't assume
That you are secure
On Christmas Eve
He'll kick in your door
Santa Claus is tapping
Your phone.

A Lawyer's Version of Christmas

Knock, knock!
Who's there?
Insanity!
Insanity who?
Do you believe Insanity
Claus?

If you want to be a lawyer when you get older, here's how you will have to talk about Christmas. Lawyers have a funny way of talking, and not just at Christmas!

Whereas, on or about the night prior to Christmas, there did occur at a certain improved piece of real property (hereinafter called "the House") a general lack of stirring by all creatures therein, including, but not limited to a mouse.

Q: What did Amaruq say after building an igloo made out of crystal clear ice?

A: "Living in a transparent igloo has its disadvantages, but you should see the murres smack it!"

A variety of foot apparel, i.e., stocking, socks and so on, had been affixed by and around the chimney in said House in the hope and/or belief that St. Nick (also known as St. Nicholas or Santa Claus; hereinafter called "Claus") would arrive at sometime thereafter.

The minor residents, i.e., the children, of the aforementioned House were located in their individual beds and were engaged in nocturnal hallucinations, i.e., dreams, wherein visions of confectionery treats, including, but not limited to, candies, nuts and/or sugar plums, did dance, cavort and otherwise appear in said dreams.

Whereupon the party of the first part (sometimes hereinafter referred to as "I"), being the joint-owner in the House with the parts of the second part (hereinafter "Mamma"), and said Mamma had retired for a long period of sleep. (At such time, the parties wore various types of headgear, e.g., kerchief and cap.)

Suddenly, and without prior notice or warning, there did occur upon the property close to said House, i.e., the lawn, a certain disruption of unknown nature, cause and/or circumstance. The party of the first part did immediately rush to a window in the House to investigate the cause of such disturbance.

At that time, the party of the first part did observe, with some degree of wonder and/or disbelief, a miniature sleigh (hereinafter called "the Vehicle") being pulled and/or drawn very rapidly through the air by approximately eight (8) reindeer. The driver of the Vehicle appeared to be and in fact was, the previously referenced Claus.

Said Claus was providing specific direction, instruction and guidance to the approximately eight (8) reindeer and specifically identified the animal co-conspirators by name: Dasher, Dancer, Prancer, Vixen, Comet, Cupid, Donner and Blitzen (hereinafter called "the Deer"). (Upon information and belief, it is further asserted that an additional co-conspirator named "Rudolph" may have been involved.)

The party of the first part witnessed Claus, the Vehicle and the Deer intentionally and willfully trespass upon the roofs of several residences located adjacent to and in the vicinity of the House, and noted that the

Q: Why are Christmas trees such bad knitters?

A: They are always dropping their needles.

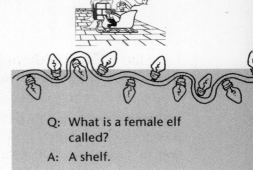

Vehicle was heavily laden with packages, toys and other items of unknown origin or nature. Suddenly, without prior invitation or permission, either

Q: What is a female elf called?

A: A shelf.

express or implied, the Vehicle arrived at the House, and Claus entered said House via the chimney.

Said Claus was clad in a red fur suit, which was partially covered with residue from the chimney, and he carried a large sack containing a portion of the aforementioned packages, toys, and other unknown items. He was smoking what appeared to be tobacco in a small pipe in blatant violation of local ordinances and health regulations.

Claus did not speak but immediately began to fill the stockings of the minor children, which hung adjacent to the chimney, with toys and other small gifts. (Said items did not, however, constitute "gifts" to said minor pursuant to the applicable provisions of the U.S. Tax Code.)

Upon completion of such task, Claus touched the side of his nose and flew, rose and/or ascended up the chimney of the House to the roof where the Vehicle and Deer waited and/or served as "lookouts." Claus immediately departed for an unknown destination.

However, prior to the departure of the Vehicle, Deer and Claus from said House, the party of the first part did hear Claus state and/or exclaim: "Merry Christmas to all, and to all a good night!"

Or words to that effect.

Respectfully Submitted,

The Grinch (also a part-time lawyer)

Whodunnit?

News Alert: An elf was found murdered in his home in the North Pole over the weekend. Detectives at the scene found the little man face down in his bathtub.

The tub was filled with milk and corn flakes, and the deceased elf had a banana protruding from his mouth.

They suspect a cereal killer.

Why So Glum, Chum?

Just before Christmas, George is fired from his job. He is standing on the railing of a high bridge getting ready to jump off, when he happens to look down and sees a little man with no arms dancing all around on the river bank below.

George thinks to himself, "Geez, my life isn't so bad after all," and he gets off the railing. He then walks down to the river bank to talk to the little man.

"Thank you," George says. "I was going to jump off that bridge and kill myself, but when I saw you dancing, even though you have no arms, I changed my mind. You saved my life."

"Dancing? I'm not dancing!" the armless man replies. "My butt itches, and I can't scratch it!"

Shhhh!

At a monastery high in the mountains in Utah, the monks have taken a vow of silence. Only at Christmastime is the vow allowed to be broken—but only by one monk, and he can say only one sentence.

Q: What do you call 10 Arctic hares hopping backwards through the snow together?

A: A receding hare line.

One Christmas Day, it is Brother Jim's turn to speak, and he stands up from the table and says, "I like the mashed potatoes we have with the turkey." He then sits down. Silence follows for 365 days.

The next Christmas during dinner, Brother Michael gets his turn to break the vow of silence, and he says, "I think the mashed potatoes are lumpy, and I hate them!"

Once again, silence for 366 days (it's leap year). The following Christmas, Brother Paul rises from the dinner table and says, "I'm fed up with this constant bickering!"

Too Much Love

Dearest John:

I went to my front door today, and the postman delivered a partridge in a pear tree from you. What a delightful gift. I couldn't have been more surprised.

With dearest love and affection, Agnes

December 15

Dearest John:

Today I received your sweet gift. Just imagine—two turtle doves! I'm touched by your thoughtful gift. They are adorable.

All my love, Agnes

December 16

Dear John:

Oh, aren't you the extravagant one! Now I must protest. I don't deserve such generosity. Three French hens! They are darling! You're much too kind.

Love, Agnes

December 17

Today the postman delivered four calling birds. Now really! They are beautiful, but don't you think enough is enough? You're being much too romantic.

Affectionately, Agnes

Too Much Love, continued

December 18

Dearest John:

What a surprise! Today I received five golden rings. One for each finger. You're impossible, but I love it. But frankly, John, all those squawking birds are beginning to get on my nerves.

All my love, Agnes

December 19

Dear John:

When I opened the door this morning, six geese a-laying were on my front porch. So you're back to the birds again, huh? Those geese are huge. Where will I ever keep them? The neighbors are complaining about the noise, and I can't sleep at night because they are so loud. Please stop!

Cordially, Agnes

December 20

John:

What's with you and those birds? Seven swans a-swimming? What kind of joke is this? There's bird do-do all over my house, and they never stop the racket. I'm a nervous wreck, and I can't sleep at night. It's not funny, so stop with those birds!

Agnes

Too Much Love, continued

December 21

Okay, Buster:

I think I prefer the birds. What am I going to do with eight maids a-milking? It's not enough with all those birds and eight maids a-milking, but they had to bring their own cows, too? There is poop all over the lawn, and I can't move around in my own house. Just lay off me.

Ag

December 22

Hey!

What are you? Some kind of sadist? Now there's nine pipers playing. And do they play! They keep chasing those maids since they got here yesterday. The cows are upset and are stepping all over those screeching birds. No wonder they screech. What am I going to do? The neighbors have started a petition to evict me. You'll get yours.

From Ag

December 23

You Creep!

Now there's 10 ladies dancing, though I don't know why I call them ladies! The cows can't sleep, and they've got diarrhea. My living room is a river of poop. The city's health inspector is taking me to court because he thinks my home should be condemned. I'm sending the police on you!

One who means it, Ag

Too Much Love, continued

December 24

Listen, Idiot:

What's with the 11 lords a-leaping? All 234 of the birds are dead. I hope you're satisfied, you rotten swine.

Your sworn enemy, Agnes McCallister

December 25

From the law offices of Taeker, Spedar and Baegar

Dear Mr. John Smith:

This is to acknowledge your latest gift of 12 drummers drumming, which you have seen fit to inflict on our client, Ms. Agnes McCallister. The destruction, of course, was total. All correspondence from you in the future will come directly to our attention. If you should attempt to reach Ms. McCallister at Happy Dale Mental Hospital, the attendants have instructions to immediately report you to the police. With this letter, please find attached a warrant for your arrest.

Merry Christmas!

Moth Man

A teenager wanders into a medical center and asks to see a doctor. The receptionist is hesitant to let him in, especially since it is Christmas Eve and she wants to go home early, but the teenager seems very agitated so she lets him in. The doctor, who has just finished seeing all his patients for the day, is in a good mood, so he agrees to see the young man.

Q: What do the sea creatures sing under the ocean during the winter?

A: Christmas corals.

The teenager enters the examination room in a rather aimless manner, and after hesitating for a second, he flops down into a chair and looks nervously around the room.

"How can I help you?" asks the doctor.

"Well, it's like this," says the teenager. "I keep thinking I'm a moth."

"A moth?"

"Yeah, I'm pretty sure I'm a moth."

"Well, I'm sorry, but you're in the wrong place, young man. What you need is a psychiatrist."

"That's what I've been thinking," replies the teenager.

"Well, as it happens, I know just the man for you," says the doctor. "I'll give him a call and see if he can see you right after Christmas."

The teenager agrees, and the doctor makes the appointment.

After the phone call, the doctor says, "Tell me something, please. It must have been very clear from the sign outside that I'm a family doctor. So if you already know you need to see a psychiatrist, why did you come in?"

"Well," the teenager says, "the door was open and the lights were on."

Let's Party!

"Are you coming to the Christmas party tomorrow night?" Billy asks his friend, Steve.

"Well," replies Steve, "I'd like to, but my pet will become very anxious if I stay away too long."

"Pet?" replies Billy. "I didn't know you had a pet. What is it?"

"A centipede."

"A centipede? That's an unusual pet. But that's no problem. Why don't you bring it with you?"

Steve agrees to take his centipede to the party.

The next evening, Billy knocks on Steve's door and finds him pacing up and down the hallway in an impatient manner.

Q: What kind of money do elves use?

A: Jingle bills.

"Ready for the Christmas party?" asks Billy.

"No, I'm not," Steve replies.

"What's the problem?"

"I'm waiting for Percy."

"Percy? Who's Percy?" asks Billy.

"My centipede," says Steven. He then turns around and says, "For goodness sake, Percy, hurry up! We'll be late for the party at this rate."

Percy does not respond.

After a few minutes, Steve calls for Percy again, but this time Steve is extremely angry. "We're fed up with waiting for you. If you don't come right away, we're leaving without you."

"Oh, shut up!" Percy replies. "You know I always have trouble getting my boots on!"

Q: What do you call a wound that is caused by being stabbed by an elf?

A: It's elf-inflicted.

Turkey Troubles

Sarah, a new young bride, calls her mother in tears. She sobs, "Oh, Mom. Richard doesn't appreciate what I do for him."

"Now, now," her mother says, trying to comfort her daughter, "I'm sure it was all just a misunderstanding."

"No, Mom, you don't understand. I bought a frozen turkey roll for our Christmas dinner, and he yelled and screamed at me about the price."

"Well, the nerve of that lousy cheapskate," says the mom. "Those turkey rolls are only a few dollars."

"No, Mother, it wasn't the price of the turkey that made him angry. It was the airplane ticket."

"Airplane ticket?" says the mom. "What did you need an airplane ticket for?"

"Well, when I read the directions on the package, it said 'Prepare from a frozen state,' so I flew to Alaska."

Bedtime Story

Santa to the elf: "What's your favorite Christmas story?"

Elf: "The one where the three creatures are scared of the Big Bad Wolf and they grow on trees!"

Santa: "Oh, you mean 'The Three Little Figs.'"

Mr. President

The vice president of the United States gives the president his daily briefing. He concludes by saying, "Yesterday, three Brazilian soldiers were killed during a Santa Claus parade."

"Oh, no!" the president exclaims. "That's terrible!"

The president's staff are stunned at his display of emotion, nervously watching as he sits quietly with his head in his hands.

Finally, the president looks up and says, "Just how many is a brazillion?"

Q: What kind of music do elves like best?

A: "Wrap" music.

Creepy Christmas

Two young boys are walking home after a Christmas party and decide to take a shortcut through the cemetery just for a laugh. Right in the middle of the cemetery they are startled by

a tap-tap-tapping noise coming from the misty shadows. Trembling with fear, they find an old man with a hammer and chisel, chipping away at one of the headstones.

"Holy cow, mister," one of the boys says after catching his breath, "you scared us half to death—we thought you were a ghost! What are you doing working here so late at night?"

"Those fools!" the old man grumbles. "They misspelled my name!"

The Blonde's Christmas Dinner

It is the first time a young blonde is making Christmas dinner for herself without her family.

She works all day trying to make the dinner just right.

The next day, her mother calls to see how everything went.

"Oh, Mother, I made myself a lovely dinner, but I had so much trouble trying to eat the turkey!" says the daughter.

"Why is that? Didn't the turkey taste good?" her mother asks.

"I don't know," replies the blonde. "It wouldn't sit still!"

Talking Parrot

Santa Claus is buying a parrot to amuse his elves while they work.

"Are you sure this parrot doesn't scream, yell or swear?" Santa asks the sales clerk in the pet store.

"Oh, absolutely. It's a religious parrot," the clerk assures him. "Do you see those strings on his legs? When you pull the right one, he recites the Lord's Prayer, and when you pull on the left, he recites the 23rd Psalm."

Q: Why didn't the tourist in the Arctic get any sleep?

A: He plugged his electric blanket into the toaster by mistake—and kept popping out of bed all night.

"Wonderful!" says Saint Nick, "but what happens if you pull both strings?"

"I fall off my perch, you fool!" says the parrot.

New Year's Nerd Resolutions

1. I will try...I will try to...I resolve to, uh...I resolve to, uh, hand my, er...I resolve to, uh, hand in my homework late!

2. I will stop checking my Facebook every half hour—every hour is much more practical.

3. When I hear a funny joke, I will not reply "LOL!"

4. I will stop sending email and Instant Messages while being on my cellphone at the same time with the same person.

5. I will try to figure out why I really need nine email addresses.

6. I will stop texting my brother who is in the next room.

7. I will not carry around six USB keys.

8. I resolve to give my brother more time to play on my Xbox.

9. I will stop watching cartoons. I'm a big boy now.

10. I won't wear suspenders anymore. They only get me more wedgies.

11. I will stop bugging my friends to check Facebook for any updates in my life.

New Year's Nerd Resolutions, continued

12. I resolve to back up my new one-terabyte hard drive daily...well, once a week...monthly, perhaps.

13. I will spend less than five hours a day on the Internet.

14. I will limit my top 10 lists to 10 items.

15. Once my zits disappear, my braces are removed and I build up some muscle, I will ask Jenny out on a date.

Talking Dog

A man in Seattle is out walking when he sees a sign in front of a house: "Talking Dog for Sale."

Q: Why did the elf put his bed into the fireplace?

A: He wanted to sleep like a log.

He decides to check it out and buy the dog as a gift for his son for Christmas. The owner of the dog tells the man that the dog is in the backyard. The guy goes to the backyard and sees a black mutt just sitting there.

"You talk?" he asks the dog.

"Sure do."

"So, what's your story?"

Q: What did the snowman order at the fast food restaurant?

A: An ice burger with chili sauce.

The dog looks up and says, "Well, I discovered my gift of speech when I was just a pup, and I wanted to help the government when I grew up, so I joined the CIA, and they flew me from country to country, sitting in rooms with spies and world leaders, because no one figured a dog would be eavesdropping. I was one of their most valuable spies for more than eight years. After that, I got a job at the airport to do some undercover security work, mostly wandering near suspicious characters and listening to their conversations. I uncovered some incredible stuff at the airport and was awarded medals for all my good work. I then got married, had a bunch of puppies and now I'm retired."

The guy is amazed. He runs back in the house and asks the owner how much he wants for the dog.

The owner says, "Ten dollars."

"Ten dollars!" says the man. "That dog is amazing. Why on earth are you selling him so cheaply?"

"'Cause he's a liar. He didn't do any of that stuff!"

Brave Guest

A generous millionaire in Los Angeles decides to throw a massive Christmas party and invites all his family and their friends. During the party at

his mansion, he grabs the microphone and announces to his guests that down the hill in the garden is a huge swimming pool with two great white sharks in it.

"I will give anything of mine to the person who is brave enough to swim across that pool," states the rich man.

The party continues with no events in the pool, until suddenly, there is a loud splash and all the guests run to the pool to see what has happened.

In the pool is a teenager who is swimming as hard as he can. The guests see shark fins come out of the water with their jaws snapping, and the guy just keeps on swimming faster. The sharks are gaining on him, but the young man manages to reach the end of the pool and gets out, exhausted and soaked.

The millionaire grabs the microphone again and says, "I am a man of my word. Anything of mine I will give to you—my Ferrari, my house, absolutely any-

Q: What is big, green and packs a trunk?
A: An elf-ephant.

thing—for you are the bravest person I have ever seen. So, young man, what will it be?"

The teenager grabs the microphone from the millionaire and says, "Why don't we start with the name of the guy who pushed me in!"

CHAPTER FIVE

Parents and Other Adults at Christmas

The awkward moment when you notice that Santa Claus has the same wrapping paper as your parents.

At the Dentist

A dad goes to his dentist's office after Christmas because something is wrong with his teeth. After a brief examination, the dentist exclaims, "Holy smoke! That plate I put in your mouth about two weeks ago is almost completely ruined! What on earth have you been eating?"

"Well, the only thing I can think of is that my wife made me some asparagus for Christmas dinner with this stuff on it. 'Hollandaise sauce' she called it, and doctor, I'm talkin' *delicious*! I've never tasted anything like it, and ever since then I've been putting the sauce on everything—meat, fish, toast, vegetables—you name it!"

"That's probably it," replies the dentist "Hollandaise sauce is made with lemon juice, which

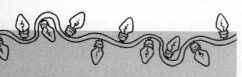

Q: Where do reindeer go to dance?

A: Christmas balls.

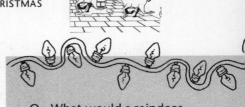

is acidic and can ruin your dentures. I'll have to make you a new plate, but made out of chrome this time."

"Why chrome?" the dad asks.

Q: What would a reindeer do if it lost its tail?

A: It would go to a "re-tail" shop for a new one.

"Well," replies the dentist, "everyone knows that there's no plate like chrome for the Hollandaise!"

Christmastime at the Airport

It's early December, and Dad's business trip in New York City has gone well, and he is ready to fly back home to Vancouver. The airport is covered with tacky, red-and-green Christmas decorations, and the loudspeakers blare annoying Christmas carols. Being someone who takes Christmas seriously, and being slightly tired, Dad is not in a particularly good mood.

While he is checking in his luggage at the ticket counter, he sees a mistletoe. It's not a real mistletoe—it's a cheap plastic one with red paint on some of the berries and green paint on the leaves.

Dad says to the woman behind the counter, "Even if I wasn't married, I wouldn't want to kiss you under that awful-looking mistletoe."

"Sir, please look more closely at where the mistletoe is placed."

Dad looks at the mistletoe and says, "Okay, I see that it's above the luggage scale, which is where you'll have to step forward for a kiss."

"That's not why the mistletoe was put there."

"No?" replies Dad. "Okay, I give up. Why is the mistletoe there?"

"So you can kiss your luggage goodbye."

School Bus Driver

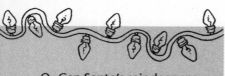

Q: Can Santa's reindeer see well in a blizzard?

A: Yes, they have excellent ice-sight.

It is Christmastime, and a school bus driver receives cards and presents from the students. Before he opens the cards, he thinks to himself, "Wow, I must be a good driver, and the kids even like me."

He opens one of the cards, and on the inside it says, "Thanks for not killing us yet. We really appreciate it."

A Memo

To: All Students

From: The Principal

Subject: School Behavior During the Christmas Season

Effective immediately, students are urged to remember the following guidelines from FROLIC

(the Federal Revelry Office and Leisure Industry Council).

1. Running aluminum foil through the principal's paper shredder to make tinsel is not allowed.
2. Playing "Jingle Bells" on your cellphone is forbidden. (It runs up an incredible long-distance bill for your parents.)
3. All corrected tests that score under 50 percent will be given the mark of "Bah Humbug."
4. Sleds are not to be used to go over the river and through the woods to Grandma's house.
5. All fruitcake has to be eaten before July 25.
6. Eggnog will not be served in the cafeteria.

In spite of all this, students are encouraged to have a Happy Holiday!

Santa in the News

Headline from the North Pole: Santa May Not Deliver Any Presents to Children in the United States This Christmas Eve.

"The U.S. Border Patrol has put such tight security around the borders, I may have problems getting into the country," Santa told reporters.

Santa, who carries no passport or other citizenship documents, could easily be detained as an illegal alien under U.S. law. "It is very risky carrying a load of toys

Q: Why was Santa's helper depressed?
A: He had low elf-esteem.

that have no country-of-origin identification," Santa added. "And my sleigh doesn't have a license plate."

Last year, Santa snuck into the U.S. through Canada. "They spotted me on their radar, and I thought for a moment I was going to get shot down by a cruise missile," Santa said. "Fortunately, it missed me."

Sources close to Santa hint that he may go online this year and send all the toys through eSanta.com. "Better hang your stockings on your computer screen this year," he said.

Letter from Martha Stewart

Dear Friends,

This perfectly delightful Christmas note is being written on paper I made myself to tell you what I have been up to. Since it snowed last night, I got up early and made a sled with old barn wood and a glue gun. I hand-painted it in gold leaf, got out my loom and made a blanket in peach and mauve. Then, to make the sled complete, I made a white horse to pull it from leftover DNA that I just had sitting around on a shelf in my craft room.

By then, it was time to start making place mats and napkins for my 20 breakfast guests. I'm serving the old standard Stewart 12-course

Q: How does Rudolph know when Christmas is coming?

A: He looks at his calen-deer.

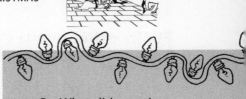

breakfast, but I'll let you in on a little secret: I didn't have time to make the table and chairs this morning, so I used the ones I had on hand.

Q: What did one piece of toast say to the other piece of toast on Christmas?

A: "'Tis the season to be jelly."

Before I moved the table into the dining room, I decided to add just a touch of the holidays. So I repainted the room in pinks and stenciled gold stars on the ceiling. Then, while the homemade bread was rising, I took antique candle molds and made the dishes (exactly the same shade of pink) to use for breakfast. These were made from Hungarian clay, which you can get in almost any neighborhood Hungarian craft store.

Well, I must run. I need to finish the buttonholes on the dress I'm wearing for breakfast. I'll get out the sled and drive this note to the post office as soon as the glue dries on the envelope I'll be making. Hope my breakfast guests don't stay too long. I have 40,000 cranberries to string before my speaking engagement at noon. It's a good thing.

Your Friend,

Martha Stewart

P.S. I made the ribbon for this ancient typewriter. I used a thin strip of gold gauze. I soaked the gauze in a mixture of white grapes and blackberries, which I picked and crushed last week just for fun.

FBI Investigation

At a clearance sale, the wife of a judge finds a green tie that is a perfect match for one of her husband's shirts. A week later, the couple is vacationing in Hawaii at Christmas to get the judge's mind off a complicated drug case. The judge notices a small, round disk sewn into the design of the tie.

When he gets home, the judge shows the disk to an FBI agent, who thinks the disk might be a "bug" planted by the men charged in the drug case. The agent sends the disk to the FBI headquarters in Washington, DC, for analysis.

Two weeks later, the judge phones the Washington office to learn the results of the tests.

"We're not sure where the disk came from," the FBI tell him, "but we discovered that when you press it, it plays 'Jingle Bells.'"

Christmas Cuts?

There was an announcement that Donner and Blitzen have decided to take the early reindeer retirement package, which has made everyone wonder whether they will be replaced. It seems as if some shopping channels, the Internet and mail-order catalogs have taken a bit of Santa's profits. So he decided to make some changes.

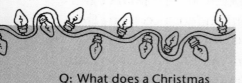

Q: What does a Christmas tree eat with?

A: Utinsels.

To make up for the loss of two reindeer, Santa bought a late model Japanese sled. Dasher and Dancer are planning to go the Harvard Business School to upgrade their skills. Rudolph's role will not be changed. Tradition still counts for something at the North Pole. Management at the North Pole denies the earlier story that said Rudolph's nose is red because of substance abuse. Some sources says it was an elf that called Rudolph "a lush who was into the sauce and never did pull his share of the load," but the elf was known to be under a lot of work stress at the time.

Knock, knock!
Who's there?
Chris!
Chris who?
Christmas!

The North Pole is continuing to look for better, more competitive ways to stay in business. Effective immediately, the following changes are to take place in the "Twelve Days of Christmas":

- The partridge will be kept, but the pear tree never made enough money. It will be replaced by a plastic hanging plant, which will save thousands of dollars in water bills.

- The two turtle doves aren't really necessary; one is enough. In addition, their romance during working hours could not be accepted. Their positions are therefore eliminated.

- The three French hens will remain. After all, everyone loves the French.

- The four calling birds will be replaced by a voice mail system, with a call-waiting option. A study will be done to see who the birds have been calling, how often and how long they talked.

- The five golden rings have been put on hold by the Board of Directors. Other less expensive precious metals will be researched.

- The six geese-a-laying is a luxury that can no longer be afforded. One egg per goose per day is not enough. Three geese will be let go, and the others better start laying faster or else.

- The seven swans-a-swimming are only decorative. Mechanical swans are on order. The current swans will have to learn some new strokes if they want to keep their position.

- The eight-maids-a-milking means that there is an imbalance of males and females in the workforce. The angry maids consider this a dead-end job with no chance to move up. The maids may have to try a-mending, a-mentoring or a-mulching.

- Nine ladies dancing has always been an odd number. This position will be phased out as the ladies start to grow older and can no longer do the fancy steps.

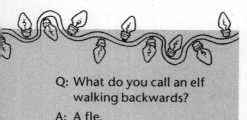

Q: What do you call an elf walking backwards?

A: A fle.

- Ten lords-a-leaping is overkill. They will be reduced to four.

- Eleven pipers piping and twelve drummers drumming is a simple case of the band getting too big. A substitution

with a string quartet, a cutback on new music and no uniforms will help reduce costs.

- We will also reduce the number of people, fowl, animals and other expenses as needed. Though incomplete, studies says that stretching deliveries over twelve days is inefficient. If we can do all this in one day, service will be improved.

Q: What do snowmen eat for breakfast?
A: Frosted Flakes.

- Regarding the lawsuit filed by the lawyer who wants to include the legal profession ("thirteen lawyers-a-suing"), we'll see him in court.

- Lastly, more cuts may be necessary in the future so that the North Pole can stay competitive. The Board will also look closely at the Snow White Division to see if seven dwarfs are really needed.

The Day After Christmas for Your Parents

'Twas the day after Christmas, and all through the house,
Every creature was hurtin', even the mouse.

The toys were all broken, their batteries dead;
Santa passed out, with some ice on his head.

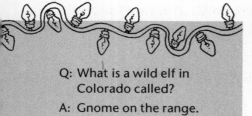

Wrapping and ribbons just covered the floor,
While upstairs, the family continued to snore.

And I in my T-shirt, new Reeboks and jeans,
I went into the kitchen and started to clean.

When out on the lawn there arose such a clatter,
I sprang from the sink to see what was the matter.

Away to the window I flew like a flash,
Tore open the curtains, and threw up the sash.

When what to my wondering eyes should appear,
But a little white truck, with an oversized mirror.

The driver was smiling, so lively and grand;
The patch on his jacket said "U.S. Postman."

With a handful of bills, he grinned like a fox,
Then quickly he stuffed them into our mailbox.

Bill after bill, after bill, they still came,
Whistling and shouting he called them by name:
"Now Dillard's, now Targets', now Penny's and Sears

Here's Visa, and Master Card, and one for the
Beer.
To the tip or your limit, every store, every mall,
Now chargeaway-chargeaway-chargeaway all!"

He whooped and he whistled as he finished his
work.
He filled up the box, and then turned with a jerk.

He sprang to his truck and he drove down the
road,
Driving much faster with just half a load.

Then I heard him exclaim with great holiday
cheer,
"Enjoy what you got—you'll be paying all year!"

Try Before You Buy

Myra is going to her
friend's Christmas party
but needs a new dress.

She goes to the mall,
stops at Gap and asks
the salesgirl, "May I try
on that dress in the
window, please?"

Q: Who says, "Oh, Oh, Oh!"?
A: Santa walking back-
wards.

"Certainly not!" says the salesgirl. "You'll have
to use the fitting room like everyone else."

What Daddy Does

Mrs. Jones, a schoolteacher, says to her class one day, "Today we'll play a spelling game before we break up for the Christmas holidays. Each of you will stand up, tell us your name, what your father does, spell what your father does and then explain his job to the class. All right, Jack, you can go first."

Q: Why do reindeer wear fur coats?

A: Because they look ridiculous in polyester.

Jack stands up and says, "My name's Jack. My father is a builder, b-u-i-l-d-e-r, and he helps to put up homes."

Mrs. Jones says, "Very good, Jack. All right, Dominic, your turn."

Dominic stands up and says, "My name's Dominic. My father's a pharmacist, f-a-m...f-a-r-n...fn..."

Mrs. Jones interrupts Dominic and says, "Dominic, you go home tonight and learn how to spell 'pharmacist.' Okay, Bobby, it's your turn."

Bobby stands up and says, "My name's Bobby. My old man is a bookie, b-o-o-k-i-e, and if he was here, he'd give you five to two odds that Dominic won't spell 'pharmacist' by tomorrow."

Twelve Days with Kids

On the 12th day of Christmas, my children gave
to me...
12 plumbers plumbing
11 diaper wipings
10 cars a-beeping
9 songs they can't sing
8 ways of belching
7 tons of washing
6 teeth decaying
5 dozen screams
4 appalling words
3 drenched friends
2 muddy gloves
and my iPod stuck in a fir tree.

Winter Driving

Young Anne has just learned to drive and leaves
work early on Christmas Eve because of the awful
winter roads. It is the worst blizzard Winnipeg has
seen in decades. She has a hard time finding her car
as she walks to the parking lot. She finally finds it,
and as the car is warm-
ing up, she wonders
whether she will make it
home in time to cele-
brate Christmas with
her family. Anne sud-
denly smiles to herself as

Q: What do you call a Santa
   that sleeps all the time?

A: Santa Snores.

she recalls her dad's advice. "If caught in a blizzard," he always told her, "follow the snowplow."

As luck would have it, a snowplow drives by at that very instant, and Anne begins to follow it.

An hour later, the snowplow parks, and the driver gets out to talk to Anne. He tells her that he noticed she has been following him for several miles. Anne smiles at the driver and tells him about her father's advice of how to drive in a blizzard.

The driver smiles back at Annie and tells her she can follow him for as long as she likes, but that he has now finished plowing the Walmart parking lot and he is moving on to Home Depot next.

In Class

It is the final examination for a history course at a high school in Montreal just before the Christmas holidays. The examination is two hours long, and exam booklets are provided. The teacher is very strict and tells the class that any exam not on his desk in exactly two hours will not be accepted, and the student will fail. A half hour into the exam, a student comes rushing in and asks the teacher for an exam booklet.

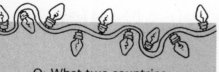

Q: What two countries should the chef use when he's making Christmas dinner?

A: Turkey and Greece.

"You're not going to have time to finish this," the teacher states sarcastically as he hands the student a booklet.

"Yes, I will," replies the student. He then takes a seat and begins writing. After two hours, the teacher calls for all the exams, and the students hand them

Q: What do snowmen do on Christmas?
A: Play with the snow angels.

in—all except the late student, who continues writing. Thirty minutes later, the last student walks up to the teacher who is sitting at his desk preparing for his next class. The student attempts to put his exam on the stack of exam booklets already there.

"No, you don't," says the teacher. "I'm not going to accept that. It's late."

The student looks incredulous and angry. "Do you know who I am?!"

"No, as a matter of fact I don't," replies the teacher.

"Do you know who I am?!" the student demands again.

"No, and I don't care," replies the teacher with an air of superiority.

"Good!" replies the student, who quickly lifts the stack of completed exams, stuffs his somewhere in the middle and walks out of the room.

Signs Your Dad Is Not Getting a Christmas Bonus

10. His co-workers refer to him as "the ghost of unemployment future."

9. The last time he saw his boss was when he testified against him in court.

8. He finds a lovely wreath of pink slips posted on his office door.

7. What he calls "my new office," everybody else calls "the supply closet."

6. The Christmas card his boss sent him says, "Don't let the door hit you on the way out."

5. He keeps getting emails reminding him that employees are required to wear pants.

4. When his boss comes over for Christmas drinks, he is crushed under an avalanche of stolen office supplies.

3. Whenever your dad asks for a raise, a guy shows up at your house and breaks his jaw.

2. In his most recent performance evaluation, the word "terrible" appeared 78 times.

1. He's the starting goaltender for the Toronto Maple Leafs.

Spending Spree

Johnny's dad leaves work one Friday afternoon just before Christmas. But it is payday, so instead of going home and using the money to buy gifts, Johnny's dad stays out the entire weekend partying with his friends and spending his entire paycheck.

When he finally goes home on Sunday night, he is confronted by his angry wife who nags him for nearly two hours about spending all that money. Finally his wife says to him, "How would you like it if you didn't see me for two or three days?"

Johnny's dad replies, "That would be fine with me."

Monday goes by and he doesn't see his wife. Tuesday and Wednesday come and go with the same results. But on Thursday, the swelling goes down just enough so that Johnny's dad can see his wife a little—out of the corner of his left eye.

Q: How long should an elf's legs be?

A: Just long enough to reach the ground.

Cultural Exchange

A man from New York City goes on a business trip to China and decides to buy a Christmas gift for his son. He walks into a shop and finds an iPod. He doesn't want to buy it if it doesn't work properly so he asks the shopkeeper, "What happens if this iPod doesn't work?"

The young shopkeeper quietly points to the only sign in English that reads, "Guarantee No Broken."

Feeling satisfied, the man pays for the iPod and returns to his hotel room. He tries to use the iPod to make sure it works, but it won't even switch on.

He quickly returns to the shop and asks for a refund or an exchange for another iPod. When the shopkeeper refuses to give either, the man points to the sign that assures him of a guarantee.

The shopkeeper then says, "Mister, you are in China. We read from the right to the left."

News Bulletin: Apple Buys Christmas!

North Pole: At a press conference held via satellite from Santa's summer estate somewhere in the Southern Hemisphere, Apple announced an agreement with Santa Claus Industries to buy Christmas. In the deal, Apple will have exclusive rights to Christmas, Reindeer and other unspecified inventions. In addition, Apple will have access to millions of households through the Santa Sleigh.

Q: How do sheep in Mexico say "Merry Christmas"?
A: Fleece Navidad.

The announcement also said that, beginning on December 9, 2013, Christmas and the Reindeer names would be copyrighted by Apple. This unusual

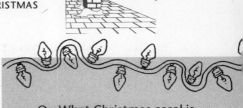

move was facilitated by the recently acquired iCourt. Apple stated that it was committed to "all who have made Christmas great," and the company vowed to "make

Q: What Christmas carol is a favorite of parents?

A: "Silent Night."

licensing of the Christmas and Reindeer names available to all. When asked, "Why buy Christmas?" CEO Tim Cook replied, "Apple has been working on a better delivery method for all of our products for some time, but we recognized that the Santa Sleigh has some immediate benefits. We'll use it first for the next release of Apple iOS and iWork."

At the press conference, the reporters were shown a video of the products that will make up the deal. The video ended with the simple Apple logo and a new iChristmas7 trademark.

Vixen, the new director of holidays and celebrations, said, "The first step is to assimilate Christmas within the Apple Organization. This will take some time, so don't expect any changes this year." She continued, "Our big plans are for next year, when we release iChristmas7. It will be bigger and better than last year." She also said that "Apple iOS users who sign up with Apple Network will get sneak previews of iChristmas8 in early November."

iChristmas7 is scheduled for release in December 2013, though one unnamed source said that it is too close to the end of the year and may slip into the first half of 2014. An economist explained that a delay would be catastrophic to next year's economy, and the nation's tax revenue, which might require that the IRS move the deadline for filing income tax returns to three months after iChristmas, whenever that was. "But it could be good in the long term," the source explained. "With Apple controlling Christmas, we may see the holiday move to May or June, which are much slower months for stores."

Q: What do you get if you cross a mistletoe and a duck?

A: A Christmas quacker.

When asked if Apple will buy other holidays, Mr. Cook explained that "iChristmas is the biggest holiday of the year, so we wanted to start there. Not all holidays are available for sale, and the others will have to show a good long-term investment." Holidays with a short history may not be in the plans.

A Santa official said that the deal was "huge, even for a man of Santa's size." Some analysts think that Santa has taken over the holiday market and is looking for a way to expand his business to year-round products and services. Other people think that the Jolly Red Man might retire in Redmond.

A spokesperson for the most famous Reindeer could not be reached for comment.

Teacher's Gift

It is Christmastime, and the grade two students in a school in Seattle decide that they will each buy their teacher a gift.

The first student, a boy whose parents own a florist shop, hands the teacher his present.

Q: Why does Santa owe everything to the elves?

A: Because he is an elf-made man.

The teacher holds it for a few seconds and then says, "I guess that it is flowers."

"How did you guess?" asks the little boy.

The teacher laughs and thanks him.

The second student, whose parents own a candy store, gives her his present.

She holds it for a few moments and then says, "I guess that is some candy."

"How did you guess?" asks the boy.

The teacher again laughs and thanks him also.

The third student, whose parents own a liquor store, gives the teacher a box, which happens to be leaking.

The teacher touches the liquid with her finger and tastes it. "Mmmm, is it white wine?" she asks.

"No," says the little girl.

So the teacher tastes it again. "Is it champagne?" she asks.

"Noooo," replies the little girl. "It's a puppy."

CHAPTER SIX

Christmas Presents

When you stop believing in Santa Claus, you start getting clothes for Christmas.

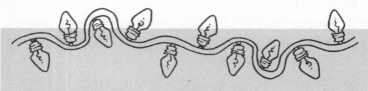

The Store Signs of Christmas

- Outside a church: "The Original Christmas Club"

- At a wedding store: "Marry Christmas"

- At a department store: "Big Pre-Christmas Sale. Come in and Mangle with the Crowd"

- At a toy store: "Ho, Ho, Ho Spoken Here"

- At a weight-loss clinic: "24 Shaping Days Until Christmas"

- In a stationery store: "For the Guy Who Has Everything...a Calendar to Remind Him When Payments Are Due"

A Christmas Story About a Rich Guy

Rick is down on his luck and is looking through the classifieds for a job. He sees an ad offering a $10-million reward to the person who finds and retrieves,

Q: What nationality is Santa Claus?

A: North Polish.

intact, something called a "tis bottle."

Having nothing to lose, he calls the man who placed the ad.

"There are only three bottles surviving in the world, and I absolutely must have this bottle," the wealthy man tells Rick. "One is deep in a jungle, one is at the bottom of a sea and one is at the top of the highest mountain. I will pay all your expenses to bring me one of these bottles, as well as giving you the $10 million."

Being an adventurous fellow and needing the money, Rick accepts the offer. He travels to a jungle in Africa and finds the bottle.

As he is walking out of the jungle, Rick is attacked by wild animals, and not only is he badly mauled, but the box containing the tis bottle goes flying, and the box and the bottle break.

After months of recovering from his injuries, he tries to retrieve the bottle at the bottom of the sea. He manages to get the second bottle, but on the way up, he is attacked by sharks and has to rush to the surface. In the hurry, Rick not only gets the bends, but the bottle falls and breaks on the boat deck. After spending two months in the hospital, he's more determined than ever to get the third and final bottle.

Rick spends a year learning mountain climbing and survival and makes the ultimate shatterproof container for the bottle. By the time he reaches the mountain top, he's weak and frostbitten, but he does not give up. He finds the last tis bottle and goes down the mountain. He spends more time in the hospital recovering from his injuries, but he keeps the bottle with him at all times.

Finally, he goes to the wealthy man's house to claim his reward and carefully unpacks the tis bottle and hands it over.

The rich man looks at the bottle and hands Rick a check for $10 million. "Thank you, and goodbye, sir," he says.

"Wait!" Rick cries, "I've spent years looking for this bottle—and almost as long in the hospital! Tell me why this bottle is so special and what it's for."

"Umm…it's a little embarrassing, actually. Why don't you just take the reward money and leave?"

"I'm not leaving here until you tell me what this bottle is for!" shouts Rick.

With a sigh, the wealthy man tells Rick to follow him to the back of his mansion. The man

Q: Elves make sandwiches with what type of bread?

A: Shortbread.

presses a hidden button to reveal a secret door.

Behind the door is a room with another door, behind a thick iron gate. The wealthy man unlocks the gate, unlocks the door and opens a heavy vault door behind it with a combination. Inside the vault are thousands of bottles neatly lined up, wall to wall and floor to ceiling, with one empty spot labeled "tis." Gently, the rich man places the bottle in its spot and says, "There you go."

Q: Why are there only snowmen and not snowwomen?

A: Because only guys are stupid enough to stand out in the snow without a coat.

"Oh, come on," Rick replies. "There has to be more to it than that."

The wealthy man picks up a delicate, padded mallet that hangs nearby and gently begins striking the bottles, and a tune emerges.

"'Tis the season to be jolly..."

Music to the Ears

"Thanks for the harmonica you gave me for Christmas," little Joshua says to his uncle the first time he sees him after the holidays. "It's the best present I ever got."

"That's great," says his uncle. "Do you know how to play it?"

"Oh, I don't play it," Joshua replies. "My mom gives me a dollar a day not to play it during the day, and my dad gives me five dollars a week not to play it at night."

For Dad

Sister: "What shall we get Dad for Christmas?"

Brother: "He says he's thinking about buying a new car..."

Sister: "Great! Let's buy him a chauffeur's outfit."

Middle Claws

Once upon a time there was a little girl named Julie who wanted a kitten for Christmas. Obviously, her parents couldn't buy a kitten and wrap it up for Christmas Day, so Julie's mother decides to buy the kitten a week before Christmas and give it to her daughter.

"You're getting your Christmas present a week early this year," her mother explains as she hands over the fluffy little kitten. "Is that what you want?"

The little girl says, "It's wonderful, Mommy... just what I wanted! But there's just one thing wrong."

"What's that, dear?" her mother asks.

"Well, it has a cute little claw on the outside of every paw and another little claw on the inside of every paw,

Q: What's white and goes up?

A: A confused snowflake.

102

but the poor little thing has no claws at all in the middle of its paws!"

Her mother smiles. "Don't worry, Julie. When you wake up on Christmas morning, you'll find the claws will be there."

Q: What did the reindeer say when he saw an elf?

A: Nothing. Reindeer can't talk.

Julie loves her kitten dearly, but she is worried about the missing claws in the middle of its paws. The days pass, and there isn't even a hint, a clue or an inkling of claws in the middle of her kitten's paws.

When Christmas Eve arrives and there is still no sign of claws, Julie goes to her mother and says, "Are you absolutely sure that the kitten will have its middle claws tomorrow? There's only a few hours to go, and there's not a hint or clue or an inkling of claws as far as I can see."

"Wait until you wake up on Christmas morning," her mother replies, smiling.

So Julie goes to sleep a worried little girl. When she wakes up on Christmas morning she ignores the presents in her stocking and rushes downstairs to look at her little kitten.

She is astounded, amazed and just a little surprised to see that her kitten has four claws on every paw! The middle ones had appeared as if by magic.

Julie runs to her parents' bedroom. "Mommy, Mommy," she says, "the kitten has grown its middle claws!"

"Of course it has," her mother says, grinning.

"But how did you know?" Julie demands.

Julie's father rolls over sleepily and says, "Oh, Julie, everybody knows that Center-claws always comes at Christmas!"

Got It All Covered

A four-year-old boy is asked to give thanks before his family's Christmas Eve dinner. The family members bow their heads and wait for the boy to start.

The young boy begins his prayer, thanking God for all his friends (naming them one by one). Then he thanks God for Mommy, Daddy, his brother, his little sister, Grandma, Grandpa and all his aunts and uncles sitting around the table.

Q: What kind of bug hates Christmas?

A: A humbug.

Then he begins to thank God for the food. He gives thanks for the turkey, the dressing, the fruit salad, the cranberry sauce, the mashed potatoes, the bread, the butter and the drinks. Then he goes on to the desserts, the pies, the cakes, even the Cool Whip.

Then the boy pauses, and everyone waits—and waits and waits.

Finally his mother tells him to go on and thank God for the broccoli (the only item he hasn't mentioned yet).

After a long silence, the young boy looks up at his mom and says, "I can't! But I know I should, so I don't know what to do!"

"What do you mean, dear?" asks his mother.

"Since it's Jesus' birthday, I bet he's listening closer than usual," replies the boy. "So if I thank God for the broccoli, he'll know that I'm lying, won't he? And then he'll tell Santa I lied! And that will mean Santa won't bring me anything!"

Q: What do vampires sing on New Year's Eve?

A: Auld Fang Syne.

Gift Idea

A 90-year-old grandmother thinks that buying presents for her family and friends was a lot of work last Christmas so she writes out checks for all of them to put in the Christmas cards she is going to send them.

In each card she carefully writes, "Buy your own present" and then mails off all the cards.

After the Christmas holidays are over, she finds all the checks under a pile of papers on her desk!

Everyone on her gift list has received a beautiful Christmas card from her that has, "Buy your own present" written inside—without a check!

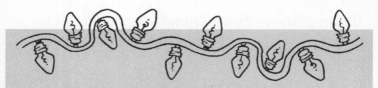

What Dad Should Never Buy Mom

10. A car wash kit.

9. A table saw.

8. Two all-day passes to *Circuit City's Home Theater Installation Seminar*.

7. A case of oil for the car.

6. A five-year subscription to *Sports Illustrated*.

5. A custom-engraved bowling ball.

4. A new outboard motor for a fishing boat.

3. All the *Die-Hard* movies on Blu-ray.

2. A new satellite dish with a sports package.

1. A three-year membership to a Weight Watchers clinic.

Surprise!

Q: What's Tarzan's favorite Christmas song?

A: "Jungle Bells."

A boy opens his Christmas present to find nothing but an empty shoebox. His parents tell him it is a Military Action Man Deserter.

Buying Something Nice

A woman from Vancouver is at a mall looking for a flannel nightgown and tries her luck in a store known for its sexy lingerie. She doesn't think she'll find the nightgown in the store, but she goes in

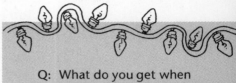

Q: What do you get when you eat Christmas decorations?
A: Tinsilitis.

anyway. To her delight, however, she finds exactly what she is looking for.

Waiting in the line to pay, the woman notices a teenager behind her holding the same flannel nightgown. This confirms what the woman has suspected all along: despite being over 50, she still has a very "with it" attitude.

"I see we have the same taste," the woman says proudly to the teenager.

"Yes," replies the teenager. "I'm getting this for my grandmother for Christmas."

Where Do Gifts Come From?

One beautiful autumn day, a mother and father are walking around in downtown Los Angeles with their son Chandler, who is five. They pass a store displaying shiny new bikes on the sidewalk. A red bike catches Chandler's eye, and he stops to look at it.

The father says, "Well, maybe Santa will bring you one for Christmas."

Chandler says, "I don't want a bike from Santa—I want one from the store!"

Guide of Gifts

You never have to figure out what to get for children, because they will tell you exactly what they want. They spend months and months researching

these kinds of things by watching Saturday-morning cartoon-show advertisements. Make sure you get your children exactly what they ask for, even if you disapprove of their choices. If your child thinks he wants Murderous Bob, the Doll with the Face You Can Rip Right Off, you'd better get it. You may be worried that it might help to encourage your child's antisocial tendencies, but believe me, you have not seen antisocial tendencies until you've seen a child who is convinced that he or she did not get the right gift.

Q: What's the best thing to give your parents for Christmas?

A: A list of everything you want.

–Dave Barry, *Christmas Shopping: A Survivor's Guide*

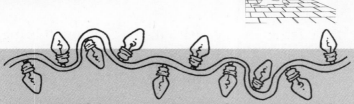

Top 10 Things to Say When Opening a Gift You Don't Like

10. "Hey! There's a gift!"

9. "Well, well, well..."

8. "Boy, it's too bad I just grew four inches, or else this would've fit."

7. "This is perfect for wearing around the basement."

6. "Gosh. I hope this never catches fire! It is fire season, ya know. There are a lot of unexplained fires."

5. "If the dog buries it, I'll be furious!"

4. "I love it, but I think all my friends will be jealous so I probably shouldn't use it."

3. "Sadly, tomorrow I enter the Federal Witness Protection Program."

2. "To think—I got this the same year I promised to give all my gifts to the poor kids."

And the number one thing to say about a Christmas gift you don't like:

1. "I really don't deserve this."

How to Wrap Christmas Presents with a Puppy in 40 Easy Steps

1. Clear a large space on table for wrapping present.
2. Go to closet and collect the shopping bag in which present is contained, and shut door.
3. Open door and remove puppy from closet.
4. Go to cupboard and get rolls of wrapping paper.
5. Go back and remove puppy from cupboard.
6. Go to drawer, and collect tape, ribbons, scissors, labels and so on.
7. Lay out presents and wrapping materials on table.
8. Go back to drawer to get string, remove puppy that has been in the drawer since last visit and collect string.
9. Remove present from bag.
10. Remove puppy from bag.
11. Open box to check present, remove puppy from box, replace present.
12. Lay out paper on table to enable cutting to size.
13. Try to smooth out paper, realize puppy is underneath and remove puppy.
14. Cut the paper to size, keeping the cutting line straight.
15. Throw away first sheet of wrapping paper because puppy has torn the paper.
16. Cut second sheet of paper to size by putting puppy in the bag the present came in.
17. Place present on paper.

How to Wrap Christmas Presents with a Puppy in 40 Easy Steps, continued

18. Lift up edges of paper to seal in the gift. Wonder why edges don't reach and realize puppy is between present and paper. Remove puppy.

19. Place a heavy object on paper, to hold in place while tearing tape.

20. Spend 20 minutes carefully trying to remove the tape from puppy with pair of nail scissors.

21. Seal the wrapping paper with tape, making corners as neat as possible.

22. Look for roll of ribbon. Chase puppy down hall in order to retrieve ribbon.

23. Try to wrap present with ribbon in a two-directional turn.

24. Re-roll ribbon and remove paper, which is now torn because of puppy's enthusiastic ribbon chase.

25. Repeat steps 13–20 until you reach last sheet of paper.

26. Decide to skip steps 13–17 in order to save time and reduce risk of losing last sheet of paper. Retrieve old cardboard box that is the right size for sheet of paper.

27. Put present in box, and tie down with string.

28. Remove sting, open box and remove puppy.

29. Put all packing materials in bag with present and head for the bathroom.

30. Once inside, lock door and start to re-lay out paper and materials.

How to Wrap Christmas Presents with a Puppy in 40 Easy Steps, continued

31. Remove puppy from box, unlock door, put puppy outside door, close and relock.

32. Repeat previous step as often as is necessary (until you can hear puppy from outside door).

33. Lay out last sheet of paper. (This will be difficult in the small area, but do your best).

34. Discover puppy has already torn paper. Unlock door, go out and hunt through various cupboards, looking for sheet of last year's paper. Remember that you haven't got any left because puppy helped with this last year as well.

35. Return to bathroom, lock door, sit on toilet and try to make torn sheet of paper look presentable.

36. Seal box, wrap with paper and repair by carefully sealing with tape. Tie up with ribbon and decorate with bows to hide worst areas.

37. Label the gift. Sit back and admire your handiwork. Congratulate yourself on completing a difficult job.

38. Unlock door, and go to kitchen to make drink and feed puppy. Spend 15 minutes looking for puppy until coming to obvious conclusion.

39. Unwrap present, untie box and remove puppy.

40. Go to store and buy gift bags.

Perfume Gift

A teenager decides that a bottle of perfume will be the perfect Christmas gift for his girlfriend. Nothing too expensive or too strong, just

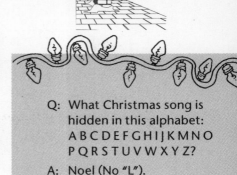

something simple. So he goes to a store and locates the cosmetics department.

Q: What Christmas song is hidden in this alphabet:
A B C D E F G H I J K M N O
P Q R S T U V W X Y Z?

A: Noel (No "L").

"I would like to buy some perfume for my girlfriend." he tells the shop assistant.

"Certainly," she replies. "Do you have anything particular in mind?"

"Not really," he says, "but nothing very expensive."

"I understand. Well, what about this one?"

"How much does it cost?"

"This one is 60 dollars."

"Hmm. That's too expensive for me," he replies.

"Very well. How about this?"

"What's the price?" he asks.

"Forty dollars."

"What else have you got?" he asks.

"Well, there's this small bottle for 20 dollars."

"Listen," he says, "what I'm really looking for is something really cheap."

The shop assistant picks up a mirror from the counter and holds it up to his face and says. "This is as cheap as you can get."

Top Gifts Mom Should Never Buy Dad

10. The *Real Housewives of Orange County* Collector's Edition with 74 minutes of extra footage.

9. Any knickknack.

8. Tickets to the ballet.

7. Another new tie.

6. A soap basket from Bath and Body Works.

5. Pajamas with teddy bears on them.

4. A vacuum cleaner.

3. A weekend seminar on "Getting in Touch With Your Feelings."

2. Pair of fuzzy bunny slippers.

1. A nose and ear hair trimmer. (Okay, well, maybe.)

Awesome Father

It is Boxing Day afternoon, and Harry goes out to meet his friends at Tim Hortons for a coffee.

His friends greet him warmly when he arrives, and soon they are discussing Christmas and sharing their stories of the festive occasion.

Then the conversation moves along to Christmas presents.

"What did you get for Christmas, Harry?" asks one of his friends.

"I got one of those iPhones," Harry replies. "They're brilliant. You can search the Internet, watch movies and take photographs—just about anything."

> Knock, knock!
> Who's there?
> Santa Ana!
> Santa Ana who?
> Santa Ana gonna bring you anything if you don't believe in him!

"Can you make phone calls?" asks one friend who is trying to be funny.

"And I bought my daughter an iPad," continues Harry. "They're better than books, you know."

"Didn't know she could read, Harry," says another friend, smiling.

"And I got my son an iPod for his music," Harry adds.

"I didn't know he could play one," says the same friend, but Harry ignores him.

"What did you get for your wife, Harry?" asks his other friend. "Something special was it?"

"I'm not sure," Harry replies. "She hasn't said anything about it yet."

"What was it?"

"Well, I got her one of those iRons."

Silly Labels on Christmas Gifts

- "The Vanishing Fabric Marker should not be used as a writing instrument for signing checks or any legal documents."

- "Do not iron while wearing shirt."

- An electric drill made for carpenters: "This product not intended for use as a dental drill."

- A cartridge for a laser printer: "Do not eat toner."

- "Never use hair dryer while sleeping."

- Warning label on a letter opener: "Caution— Safety goggles recommended."

- On a child's buggy: "Remove child before folding."

- A baby-stroller featuring a small storage pouch: "Do not put child in bag."

- A dishwasher: "Do not allow children to play in the dishwasher."

- A manufactured fireplace log: "Caution—Risk of fire."

- "If you do not understand, or cannot read, all directions, cautions and warnings, do not use this product."

The Girl Knows What She Wants

Santa is used to kids bringing their lists with them when they visit him. But one little girl really knows what she wants and how to get it.

The girl, about six years old and dressed in her frilliest dress, sits on Santa's lap and proceeds to read more than 20 items off her list—everything from Barbie dolls to a particular brand of baby carriage.

As the little girl reaches the end of her list, she looks up at Santa and says, "If you can't bring all of this, don't worry. My daddy will give it to me."

"Do you want to give me the list?" Santa asks.

"No, I think I should keep it for my daddy," she replies.

Santa quickly agrees.

From Santa

Alex is five, and all his Christmas presents are always signed, "From Santa."

Knock, knock!
Who's there?
Donut!
Donut who?
Donut open until Christmas Day!

After Alex has opened all his presents on Christmas morning, his parents become aware that he is looking quite sad for no obvious reason.

"What's the matter, Alex?" his father asks.

"Ummm," replies Alex slowly, "I was really hoping that you and Mommy would give me something for Christmas."

117

Secret Santa

An old man walks into a post office one day and sees a young kid with an evil smirk on his face standing at the counter methodically placing cards that say "Merry Christmas, My Love!" on beautifully wrapped presents. The boy then takes out a perfume bottle and starts spraying scent all over the cards.

The guy's curiosity gets the better of him, so he goes up to the kid and asks him what he is doing. The kid says, "I'm sending out 100 Christmas presents that are signed, 'Guess who?'"

"But why?" asks the guy.

"I'm a kid. Love is icky," the boy replies.

Wrong Gift, Dude!

Bob is in trouble. He forgot it is Christmas. His mom is really angry.

She tells him, "Tomorrow morning, I expect to find a gift in the driveway that goes from 0 to 200 in six seconds, and it better be there!"

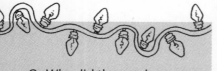

Q: Why did the candy cane cross the road?

A: Because it wanted to get a licking.

The next morning Bob gets up early and leaves for school. When his mom wakes up, she looks out the window, and sure enough, there is a gift-wrapped box in the middle of the driveway.

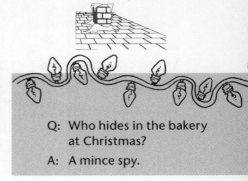

Confused, she puts on her bathrobe, runs out to the driveway and takes the box into the house. She opens the box and finds a brand-new bathroom scale.

Q: Who hides in the bakery at Christmas?

A: A mince spy.

Bob has been missing since Friday.

In Your Dreams

On Christmas morning, a girl calls her boyfriend and says, "I just dreamed that you gave me a beautiful diamond necklace. What do you think it means?"

"You'll know tonight," he replies and smiles to himself.

That evening, the teenager arrives at his girlfriend's home with a package and gives it to her.

Delighted, she opens the box, only to find a book entitled *The Meaning of Dreams*.

CHAPTER SEVEN

Holiday Specials

It's beginning to cost a lot like Christmas.

Good Manners

A store's Santa Claus gives little Jeanie a candy cane. Her mother says, "What do you say, Jeanie?"

Jeanie looks up at Santa and says, "Charge it!"

Shopping for Dads

Buying gifts for dads isn't nearly as complicated as it is for moms.

But don't worry…this list of rules will answer all your gift-giving questions for dad.

Rule 1: When in doubt, buy him a cordless drill. It does not matter if he already has one. My friend's dad owns 17 and never complains about the gifts. Your dad can never have too many cordless drills. No one knows why.

Rule 2: If you cannot afford a cordless drill, buy your dad anything with the word "ratchet" or "socket" in it. Dads love saying those two words. "Hey, George,

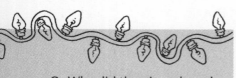

Q: Why did the gingerbread man go to the doctor?

A: He was feeling crummy.

can I borrow your ratchet?" "Okay. By the way, are you through with my 3/8 inch socket yet?" Again, no one knows why.

Rule 3: If you are really, really broke, buy your dad anything for his car. A 99-cent ice scraper, a small bottle of de-icer or something to hang from his rear-view mirror. Dads love gifts for their cars. No one knows why.

> Q: What do babies wants for Christmas?
> A: All their teeth!

Rule 4: Do not buy your dad socks. Or ties. And never buy bathrobes.

Rule 5: Buy your dad a new remote control to replace the one he has worn out. If you have a lot of money, buy the old man a big screen TV with the little picture in the corner. Watch him go ape wild as he flips and flips and flips. Your entertainment will be watching him have fun!

Rule 6: Do not buy him industrial-sized canisters of after-shave or deodorant. Especially Old Spice.

Rule 7: Buy label makers. (They're almost as good as buying a cordless drill.) Within a couple of weeks, you'll find labels absolutely everywhere that say, "Socks," "Shorts," "Cups," "Bowls," "Door," "Lock," "Sink." You get the idea. No one knows why.

Rule 8: Never buy your dad anything and then tell him he should read the instructions because the box says, "Some assembly required." It will ruin Christmas. He will always have parts left over.

Q: What disasters could happen if you dropped the Christmas turkey?

A: The downfall of Turkey, the breakup of China and the over-throw of Greece.

Rule 9: Good places to shop for dad include Northwest Iron Works, Parr Lumber, Home Depot, John Deere, Valley RV Center and Les Schwab Tire. (NAPA Auto Parts and Sear's Clearance Centers are also excellent choices.)

It doesn't matter if he doesn't know what the gift is for. "From NAPA Auto? Must be something need. Hey! Isn't this a starter for a 1968 Mustang? Wow! Thanks!"

Rule 10: Dads enjoy danger. That's why they never cook—but they will barbecue. Get your dad a monster barbecue with a 100-pound propane tank. Tell him the gas line leaks. "Oh, the thrill! The challenge! Who wants a hamburger?"

Rule 11: Tickets to a New York Giants game are a smart gift. However, he will not appreciate tickets to a lecture on "The History of 19th-Century Quilts." Everyone knows why.

Rule 12: Dads also love chain saws. Never, ever, buy him a chain saw, however. If you don't know why, refer to Rule 7. (Remember what happens when he gets a label maker?)

Rule 13: It's hard to beat a really good wheelbarrow or an aluminum extension ladder. Never buy a stepladder. It must be an extension ladder. No one knows why.

Rule 14: Rope. Dads love rope. It takes them back to their cowboy origins, or at least the Boy Scouts. Nothing says "I love you" like 100 feet of strong rope. No one knows why.

Have fun shopping!

Politically Correct Christmas

'Twas the night before Christmas, and Santa was a wreck...

How to live in a world that's politically correct?

His workers no longer would answer to "Elves,"

"Vertically Challenged" they were calling themselves.

And labor conditions at the North Pole

Were alleged by the union to stifle the soul.

Four reindeer had vanished, without much propriety,

Released to the wilds by the Humane Society.

And equal employment had made it quite clear

That Santa had better not use just reindeer.

So Dancer and Donner, Comet and Cupid,

Were replaced with four pigs, and you *know* that looked stupid!

The runners had been removed from his sleigh;

Q: Did you hear about the cracker's Christmas party?

A: It was a BANG.

The ruts were termed dangerous by the EPA.

And people had started to call for the cops
When they heard sled noises on their roof tops.
Second-hand smoke from his pipe had his work-
ers quite frightened.
His fur-trimmed red suit was called "Unenlight-
ened."
And to show you the strangeness of life's ebbs
and flows,
Rudolf was suing over unauthorized use of his
nose
And had gone on the *Ellen* show, in front of the
nation,
Demanding millions in over-due compensation.

So, half of the reindeer were gone; and his wife,
Who suddenly said she'd enough of this life,
Joined a self-help group, packed and left in a whiz,
Demanding from now on her title was "Ms."
And as for the gifts, why, he'd ne'er had a notion
That making a choice could cause so much com-
motion.

Nothing of leather,
nothing of fur,
Which meant nothing
for him. And noth-
ing for her.

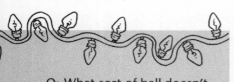

Q: What sort of ball doesn't
bounce?
A: A snowball.

Nothing that might
be construed to pol-
lute.

Nothing to aim.
Nothing to shoot.

Nothing that clam-
ored or made lots of
noise.

Knock, knock!
Who's there?
Mary!
Mary who?
Merry Christmas!

Nothing for just girls. Or just for the boys.

Nothing that claimed to be gender specific.

Nothing that's warlike or non-pacific.

No candy or sweets...they were bad for the tooth.

Nothing that seemed to embellish a truth.

And fairy tales, while not yet forbidden,

Were like Ken and Barbie, better off hidden.

For they raised the hackles of those psychological

Who claimed the only good gift was one eco-
logical.

No baseball, no football...someone could get
hurt;

Besides, playing sports exposed kids to dirt.

Dolls were said to be sexist, and should be passé;

And Nintendo would rot your entire brain away.

So Santa just stood there, disheveled, perplexed;

He just could not figure out what to do next.

He tried to be merry, tried to be gay,

But you've got to be careful with *that* word these
days.

His sack was quite empty, limp to the ground;
Nothing fully acceptable was to be found.
Something special was needed, a gift that he might
Give to all without angering the left or the right.
A gift that would satisfy, with no indecision,
Each group of people, every religion;
Every ethnicity, every hue,
Everyone, everywhere…even *you*!
So here is that gift, it's price beyond worth…
"May you and your loved ones enjoy peace on earth."

Take That!

A grandfather buys a train set by mail order as a Christmas present for his grandson.

The toy arrives in 189 pieces. The instructions say that it could be put together in an hour. However, it takes the old man two days to build the train set.

Finally, when it is all put together, he writes a check, cuts it into 189 pieces and mails it to the company.

Q: Why did Santa Claus take his Christmas tree to the dentist?

A: To get a root canal.

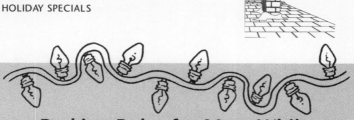

Parking Rules for Mom While Christmas Shopping

1. When waiting for a parking spot, stop in the middle of the road, don't signal and park your car diagonally to prevent other vehicles from passing.

2. Always park on the lines, taking up as many spots as possible. Diagonal parking is preferred.

3. In a crowded parking lot, if you find a spot and have the opportunity to pull through to an adjacent one, drive up halfway and stop on the line, taking both spots.

4. As you pull into a spot, if you see that the space ahead of you is empty and another driver is signaling to take it, pull through and grab that spot.

5. Always park close enough so that the other driver in the next vehicle must grease up with Vaseline to squeeze into his or her car.

6. When getting out of your car, hit the vehicle next to you with your door.

7. When driving through the parking lot, ignore the painted lanes and drive diagonally from one end to another at a high rate of speed.

8. Stop in front of a store while waiting to pick up a friend, and make sure you park in the middle of the road so no other vehicle can pass. Also do this when you drop off passengers.

9. When a vehicle from the opposite direction is signaling and waiting for a parking space, position your car so that you are in his way and let the car behind you take it.

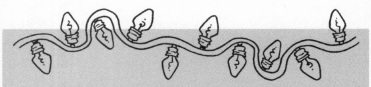

New Year's Resolutions Your Mom Will Probably Never Keep

- When she hears a funny joke, she will not reply, "LOL, LMAO, or ROTFLMAO!"

- Start using Facebook for something other than Farmville and stupid quizzes.

- Figure out why she really needs five Facebook accounts.

- Stop tagging pictures of herself in pictures on Facebook even when she's not in them.

- Spend less than $1000 for coffee at Starbucks.

- Lose 20 pounds by going to the gym.

- Stop repeating herself again, and again, and again.

- Think of a password other than "password."

Pedro Wants a Weeweechu

During a romantic full moon, young Pedro says to his girlfriend, "Hey, *mamacita*, let's do Weeweechu."

"Oh no, not now. Let's look at the moon!" replies Rosita.

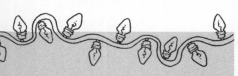

Q: How do snowmen travel around?

A: By iceycle (bicycle).

"Oh, c'mon baby, let's you and I do Weeweechu. I love you, and it's the perfect time," Pedro begs.

"But I just wanna hold your hand and watch the moon," says Rosita.

"Please, *corazoncito*, just once, do Weeweechu with me."

Rosita looks at Pedro and says, "Okay, one time, we'll do Weeweechu."

Pedro grabs his guitar, and they both start to sing: "Weeweechu a Merry Christmas, Weeweechu a Merry Christmas, Weeweechu a Merry Christmas, and a Happy New Year!"

Knock, knock!
Who's there?
Abbey!
Abbey who?
Abbey New Year!

Holiday Singing

A week before Christmas, little Freida decides to go out caroling in her neighborhood one night.

She knocks on the door of a house and begins to sing. A man with a violin in his hand answers the door.

Within a minute, tears are streaming down the man's face! Freida goes on singing for half an hour. She sings every carol she knows, and some she doesn't.

As last she stops. "I understand," she says softly when she sees the man's tears. "You are remembering the happy Christmas days when you were young. You're a sentimentalist."

"No," the man snivels. "I'm a musician!"

The Tree Tradition

Q: What does Santa suffer from if he gets stuck in a chimney?

A: Santa Claustrophobia.

Santa is very angry. It is Christmas Eve, and *nothing* is going right. Mrs. Claus has burned all the cookies. The elves are complaining about not getting paid for the overtime they did while making the toys. The reindeer have been eating all afternoon and are dead tired. And to make matters worse, they took the sleigh out for a spin earlier in the day and crashed it into a tree.

Santa is furious. "I can't believe it! I've got to deliver millions of presents all over the world in just a few hours—all of my reindeer are asleep, the elves are on strike and I don't even have a Christmas tree! I sent that stupid Little Angel out hours ago to find a tree, and he isn't even back yet! What am I going to do?"

Just then, the Little Angel opens the front door and steps in from the snowy night, dragging a Christmas tree. He says, "Yo, fat man! Where do you want me to stick the tree this year?"

And thus the tradition of angels atop Christmas trees came to pass.

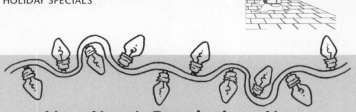

New Year's Resolutions Your Dad Can Actually Keep

- Read less.
- Start buying lottery tickets at a luckier store.
- Stop exercising. Waste of time. Watch more TV.
- Watch less TV in standard definition.
- Gain enough weight to get on *The Biggest Loser.*
- Watch more football.
- Start washing his hands after using the bathroom.
- Do less laundry, and use more deodorant.
- Not waste time reliving the past. Instead, he'll spend more time worrying about the future.
- Stop buying worthless junk on Ebay, because QVC has better specials.
- Spend more time at work.
- Stop bringing lunch to work. Eat out more.

Food Tips at Christmas

1. Carrot sticks. Two words: avoid them. Anyone who puts carrots out for a snack for their guests knows nothing of the Christmas spirit. In fact, if you see carrots, leave immediately. Go next door, where they're serving chocolate cake.

2. Drink as much soda pop as you can. It's Christmas!

3. If something comes with gravy, use it. That's the whole point of gravy. Pour it on. Make a volcano out of your mashed potatoes. Fill it with gravy. Eat the volcano. Repeat.

4. Eat as much as you can while the going is good. The whole point of a Christmas party is to eat other people's food for free. Lots of it.

5. Under no circumstances should you exercise between Christmas and New Year's. This is the time for sitting on the couch and watching as much TV as you can.

6. If you come across something really good at your Grandma's, like frosted Christmas cookies in the shape and size of Santa, stand next to them and don't move. Eat as many as you can before your mom or dad drags you away. You can't leave any cookies behind. You're not going to see them again until next year. ☞

Food Tips at Christmas, continued

7. Same for pies. Apple. Pumpkin. Mincemeat. Have a slice of each. Or, if you don't like mincemeat, have two pieces of apple pie and one of pumpkin. Always have three slices. When else do you get to have more than one dessert?

8. Did someone mention fruitcake? Avoid it at all costs.

9. And one final tip: If you don't feel terrible when you leave a party or get up from the table, you haven't been paying attention. Reread tips. Start over. But hurry! Cookieless January is just around the corner.

Mmmm, Turkey

It is Christmas Eve, and Laura and her mom are shopping for a turkey in a supermarket. There are only a few turkeys left, and Laura's mom wants a large one for her family of seven.

Q: What kind of bird can write?

A: A pen-guin.

In desperation, Laura's mom calls over a shop assistant and says to him, "Excuse me. Do these turkeys get any bigger?"

"No," he replies, "they're all dead."

On Sale

One day a dad is driving home when he suddenly realizes that it is close to Christmas and he hasn't bought his daughter a gift. Out of the corner of his eye, he notices a shopping mall. Knowing that it is "now or never," he quickly pulls his car through three lanes of traffic, finds a parking spot and runs into the mall.

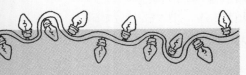

Q: What did Adam say on the day before Christmas?

A: It's Christmas, Eve.

After a frantic search, he finds a toy store, goes inside and attracts the attention of the store clerk. When he is asked what he'd like, the man simply says, "A Barbie doll."

The shop assistant looks at him and says, "So which Barbie would that be?"

The man looks surprised, so the assistant says, "We have 'Barbie Goes to the Ball' at $19.99, 'Barbie Goes Shopping' at $19.99, 'Barbie Goes Clubbing' at $19.99, 'Barbie Goes to the Gym' at $19.99, 'Cyber Barbie' at $19.99 and 'Divorced Barbie' at $249.99."

The man can't help himself and asks, "Why does Divorced Barbie cost $249.99 when all those other Barbies are selling for $19.99?"

"Well, sir, that's quite obvious!" says the assistant. "Divorced Barbie comes with Ken's house, Ken's car, Ken's furniture..."

Signs Your Parents Bought a Lousy Tree

- It's two feet tall and forty-feet wide.

- Salesman's opening line to your dad: "You're not a cop, are you?"

- The tree looks suspiciously like a broom handle with a lot of coat hangers.

- Each branch has "Duraflame" printed on it.

- It's green, very small and says "Air Freshener" on it.

- Rabbis have better Christmas trees than your family.

- Your dad constantly brags about the tree's "trunk size."

The Three Stages of Being a Father

1. He believes in Santa Claus.
2. He doesn't believe in Santa Claus.
3. He *is* Santa Claus.

Signs You're Sick of the Holidays

8. You've got red and green bags under your eyes.

7. You're serving reindeer potpie.

6. When you hear, "Sleigh bells ring, are you listenin'?" you scream, "No! I'm not listening!"

5. You climb on your roof and start shooting carolers with your air gun.

4. You think you hear your Christmas tree taunting you.

3. Instead of spending time with your family, you'd rather watch a guy paint the walls.

2. Eggnog is coming out of your ears.

1. Two words: tinsel rash.

The Perfect Tree

Q: Where do snowmen go to dance?

A: Snowballs.

Two young blonde women are two hours from Boulder, Colorado, and are walking deep in the forest searching for a Christmas tree. They are warmly dressed from head to toe and are carrying a saw, a hatchet

and a rope to drag the Christmas tree back to the car.

The two blondes are so determined to find the perfect Christmas tree that they search for hours, slugging through knee-deep snow and blowing wind, and they aren't even distracted!

Q: What do you get if you cross an apple and a Christmas tree?
A: Pineapple.

Finally, five hours pass, and the sun is beginning to set, so one blonde turns to the other and says, "I give up! I can't take this anymore! There are hundreds of beautiful Christmas trees all around us. Let's just cut one down whether it's decorated or not!"

Christmas Diet

Young Reginald is terribly overweight after Christmas, so his doctor places him on a strict diet.

"I want you to eat regularly for two days, then skip a day, and repeat this procedure for two weeks. The next time I see you, you'll have lost at least five pounds," his doctor assures him.

When Reginald returns to his doctor after two weeks, he shocks his doctor by having lost almost 20 pounds.

"Why, that's amazing," the doctor says, greatly impressed. "You certainly must have followed my instructions."

Reginald nods and says, "Yes, but I'll tell you what, though. I thought I was going to drop dead on the third day."

"Why? From hunger?" asks his doctor.

"No, from all that skipping!"

Pudding Problems

Martha is a young girl who decides during Christmas to try the delights of microwave cooking for the first time.

She gets out her mom's Christmas pudding recipe and assembles all the ingredients. She follows her mom's tradition of getting each member of the family to stir the mixture "for luck." When Martha reads the microwave's manual for the cooking time, she doesn't believe that 10 minutes is enough time to cook the pudding, so she decides to add an extra 30 minutes. She then goes to watch TV.

Q: What's a good holiday tip?

A: Never catch snowflakes with your tongue until all the birds have gone south for the winter.

While Martha is in the living room watching her favorite cartoon, she doesn't see the pudding spitting in the microwave oven, nor does she hear all the mini-explosions. When she finally goes into the kitchen, the pudding smells like burnt sugar and looks like a ball of tar. Naturally, the Christmas pudding is a disaster— Martha can't even poke it with a fork. In fact, the

black ball sticks to the bottom of the bowl, and her dad has to use a screwdriver to get it out.

In a fit of anger, Martha throws the shriveled Christmas pudding to Togo, her St. Bernard puppy. After a few days, Martha is able to see the funny side, and Togo loves his new indestructible toy, which he plays with until the next Christmas.

Parents at a Party

Bobby's parents aren't too smart. For example, one night last December, Bobby attended a fancy Christmas party with his parents. The conversation soon turned to Mozart. "Absolutely brilliant, lovely...oh, a fine fellow...a genius, Mozart was," says one of the guests.

Bobby's mom, wanting to get in on the conversation remarks, "Ah, Mozart. You're so right. It was just this morning that I saw him getting on the number 20 bus going downtown."

There is a sudden hush, and all eyes turn toward her. Her husband pulls her aside and angrily says, "We're leaving right now!"

In the car on the way home, Bobby's mom turns to her husband and says, "You're really mad about something, aren't you?"

"How could you tell? My goodness! I've never been so embarrassed in my life! You saw Mozart take the number 20 bus downtown, huh? Everybody knows that the number 20 bus doesn't go downtown!"

10 Uses for that Awful Fruitcake

1. Use it as a doorstop.

2. Use it as a paper weigh.

3. Use it as boat anchor.

4. Use as bricks in fireplace.

5. Hold up your bike when changing tires.

6. Use it to hold up the Christmas tree.

7. Use as a pencil holder.

8. Give it to the cat for a scratching post.

9. Put it in the backyard to feed the birds and squirrels.

10. Keep it until summer—you can weigh down your tent when you go camping.

CHAPTER EIGHT

Family Christmas

Christmas: The time when everyone gets Santamental.

Stockings

'Twas the night before Christmas and all through the house,

Not a creature was stirring, not even a mouse.

The stockings were hung by the chimney with care.

They'd been worn all week and needed the air.

A Diamond Ring

A guy buys his wife a beautiful diamond ring for Christmas.

After hearing about this extravagant gift, a friend of his says, "I thought she wanted one of those sporty four-wheel-drive vehicles."

Q: How would you fire Santa?

A: Give him the sack.

"She did," he replies. "But where was I going to find a fake Jeep?"

Breakfast in Bed

On Christmas Day, a little boy decides to make his dad breakfast in bed. He brings his dad cereal, toast and coffee and says, "Try the coffee, Dad."

The dad takes a sip of the coffee and nearly passes out because it is so strong.

The little boy asks, "How do you like it, Dad?"

The dad doesn't want to hurt his son's feelings so he says, "This is…something else. I've never tasted coffee quite like this before, son."

The little boy smiles from ear to ear and says, "Drink some more, Pops."

As the dad chokes down the coffee, he notices two little army men in the bottom of the cup, and says, "Hey! Why did you put army men in here?"

The little boy again smiles and sings, "The best part of waking up, is soldiers in your cup."

An Axe to Grind

A boy begs his father to buy a real Christmas tree this year. Each year, the boy asks and the father tells him, "I don't want to pay for it." But the son keeps begging. Unable to bear his son's whining, he picks up his axe one day and heads out of the house.

Thirty minutes later, he returns with a great big Christmas tree.

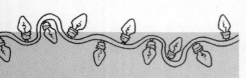

Q: What's red and white and gives presents to good little fish on Christmas?

A: Sandy Claws.

"How did you cut it down so fast?" his son asks.

"I didn't cut it down," the father replies. "I got it at a tree lot."

Q: What do you get when you cross an archer with a gift-wrapper?

A: Ribbon hood.

"Then why did you bring an axe?"

"Because I didn't want to pay."

Merry Christmas!

Little girl: Why do we wish people a "Merry Christmas" instead of a "Happy Christmas"?

Grandpa: The two are about the same, but if you say "Merry Christmas," an extra twinkle is seen in the eyes.

Mom's Prank

On Christmas Day, my family is at my older sister's house for the holiday feast. Knowing how gullible my sister is, my mom decides to play a trick. She tells my sister that she needs something from the store and asks my sister to go to get it.

When my sister leaves the house, Mom takes the turkey out of the oven, removes the stuffing, then takes a Cornish hen and inserts it into the turkey. She then places the bird(s) back into the oven.

When it's time for dinner, my sister pulls the turkey out of the oven and starts to remove the stuffing. When her serving spoon hits something, she reaches in and pulls out the smaller bird. With a look of total shock on her face, my mother exclaims, "Barbara, you've cooked a pregnant bird!"

At the reality of this horrifying news, my sister starts to cry hysterically. It takes the entire family almost two hours to convince her that turkeys lay eggs!

And yes, my sister is a blonde!

Q: Why does Scrooge love all of the reindeer?

A: Because every buck is dear to him.

Who Kissed Santa?

At Sarah's elementary school Christmas concert, the first-grade girl introduces the song she will be singing: "I Saw Mommy Kissing Santa Claus." In a clear and loud voice, Sarah sings, "Oh, what Mommy would have thought if she saw Daddy kissing Santa Claus!"

With What!

Billy: I don't think I want Christmas dinner tonight.

John: Why is that?

Billy: My mom gave me a haircut this morning. And now she says she's going to make Christmas dinner with all the trimmings!

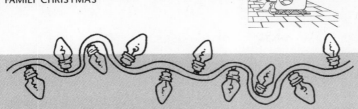

Christmas Insults for the Playground

- He's a couple of slates short of a full roof.
- He's a few pies short of a holiday.
- She has a few too many lights out in her Christmas tree.
- He's all wax and no wick.
- Her batteries are not included.
- He's as bright as Alaska in December.
- His chimney's clogged.
- He got his brains as a stocking stuffer.
- She's not the brightest bulb on the Christmas tree.
- He's several nuts over fruitcake minimum.
- She's a few presents short of a full sleigh.

Christmas Rush

Max comes home to his wife Minnie on Christmas Eve and says, "I left the mall in such a hurry today that I forgot to get two things."

Knock, knock!
Who's there?
Holly!
Holly who?
Holly-days are here again!

"Like what?" Minnie asks.

"For one thing," Max says, "I forgot to get wrapping paper."

"That's okay," Minnie says. "You don't need to wrap my present."

"Actually," Max says, "that's the other thing."

Swear Words

A seven-year-old tells his four-year-old brother that they should start swearing. "When we go downstairs for breakfast on Christmas morning, I'll say 'hell' and you say 'damn it.'"

The four-year-old happily agrees.

At breakfast, the seven-year-old says, "Aw, hell, Mom, I'll just have some toast."

The surprised mother quickly smacks him. The boy runs upstairs crying.

The mother then turns to the younger boy and says, "And what would *you* like for breakfast?"

"I don't know," the four-year-old blubbers, "but, damn it, it's not gonna be toast!"

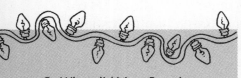

Q: What did Mary Poppins want from Santa?

A: Supercalifragilistic-expialisnowshoes.

Backseat Driver

My parents get along just great, except that my mom is a "backseat driver." After years of putting up

with her pestering, my dad has finally decided he has had enough and he tells her that he is no longer driving with her in the car. One day, while Dad and I are on our way to the mall to do some Christmas shopping, his cellphone rings as he is pulling into the parking lot. It's my mom calling him.

By chance, she has entered the parking lot right behind us.

"Honey," my mom says through the speaker phone, "your turn signal is still on. And put on the windshield wipers; it's starting to snow!"

Q: What do you get when you cross a snowman with a vampire?

A: Frostbite.

Wishful Thinking

The Santa Claus at a mall in Las Vegas is very surprised when a young woman about 20 years old walks up and sits on his lap. Santa doesn't usually take requests from adults, but she smiles nicely at him, so he asks her, "What do you want for Christmas?"

"Something for my mother, please," says the young lady.

"Something for your mother? Well, that's very thoughtful of you," says Santa. "What do you want me to bring her?"

Without blinking an eye, she replies, "A son-in-law!"

Gobble, Gobble

It's the day before Christmas, and a butcher in Calgary is just locking up his store when a man begins pounding on the front door.

"Please let me in," says the man desperately. "I forgot to buy a turkey, and my wife will kill me if I don't come home with one."

Q: What is invisible and smells like milk and cookies?

A: Santa's burps!

"Okay," says the butcher. "Let me see what I have left." He goes into the freezer at the back of the store and discovers that there's only one scrawny turkey left. He brings it out to show the man.

"That one is too skinny. What else you got?" asks the man.

The butcher takes the bird back into the freezer and waits a few minutes then brings out the same turkey to the man.

"Oh, no," says the man. "That one doesn't look any better. You better give me both of them!"

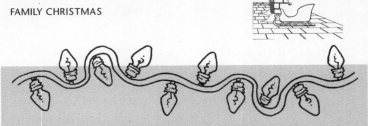

You Know You Overdid Christmas Dinner When...

- Paramedics bring in the Jaws of Life to pry you off the couch.
- A guest quotes a Biblical passage from "The Feeding of the 5000."
- The gravy boat your mom set out was a real 12-foot boat.
- You receive a sumo wrestler application in your email.
- You set off three earthquake seismographs while walking to school.
- Accidently pricking your finger produces gravy.
- That rash on your stomach turns out to be a burn from sitting at the dining room table too long.
- Representatives from the Butterball Hall of Fame call twice.

Teacher's Pet

Imagine the fourth grade teacher's joy when she and her students are getting out the Christmas decorations and find a present from one of her students that she forgot to open last year. The students' excited faces are pictures of happiness as she unwraps the gift and opens the box. Such a pity it was a puppy.

Tree Shopping

Some of my favorite memories involve my family's annual trips to the local Christmas-tree farm. Although we have an artificial tree at our house, my parents still go with my grandparents when they cut down their tree.

When my mom announced we would be helping them pick a tree the next day, I expected my six-year-old sister to be excited about the outing.

Instead, she furrowed her brow, puzzled, and asked, "What did they do with the one we got them last year?"

Smart Parents

An old man in Phoenix calls his son in New York two days before Christmas and says, "I hate to ruin the holidays for you and the kids, son, but I have to tell you that your mother and I are getting a divorce."

"Dad, what are you talking about?" the son screams.

Q: Why did Jimmy's grades drop after the holidays?

A: Because everything was marked down.

"We can't stand the sight of each other any longer," the father says. "We're sick of each other, and I'm sick of talking about this, so you call your sister in Chicago and tell her."

> Q: What did the bald man say when he got a comb for Christmas?
>
> A: Thanks. I'll never part with it.

Frantic, the son calls his sister, who explodes on the phone. "There's no way they're getting divorced," she shouts. "I'll take care of this."

She calls Phoenix immediately and screams at her father, "You are *not* getting divorced. Don't do a single thing until I get there. I'm calling my brother back, and we'll all be there tomorrow with the kids. Until then, don't do a thing, do you hear me?" and hangs up.

The old man hangs up the phone, turns to his wife and says, "Okay, it's done. They're bringing the grandkids for Christmas, and they're also paying their own way!"

New and Improved

Over the Christmas holidays, Molly is sitting on her grandpa's lap as he reads the newspaper, not paying any attention to her. So she starts studying the wrinkles on his old face. She gets up the nerve and rubs her fingers over the wrinkles and then over her own face and looks puzzled.

She finally asks, "Grandpa, did God make you?"

"He sure did, honey, and it was a long, long time ago," he replies with a smile.

"Well, did God make me?" she asks.

"Yes, he did, and that wasn't too long ago," he answers.

The little girl thinks for a minute and then says, "Wow! He's sure doing a lot better job these days, isn't he!"

Brotherly Love

Randy has been listening to his sister practicing her singing all day, for several days.

"Sis," he says, "I wish you'd sing Christmas carols."

"That's so nice of you to say, Randy," she replies. "But why?"

"Then I'd only have to hear you once a year!"

Searching for Jesus

A Sunday School teacher of pre-schoolers is concerned that his students might be a little confused about Jesus Christ because of the Christmas season emphasis on his birth. He wants to make sure they understand that the birth of Jesus occurred a very long time ago. He wants to be sure they know that Jesus grew up and did many things.

Q: Which of Santa's reindeer has bad manners?

A: Rude-olph.

152

So he asks his class, "Where is Jesus today?"

Sam raises his hand and says, "He's in heaven."

Mary is then called on and says, "He's in my heart."

Q: Why did the elves ask the turkey to join their band?

A: Because the turkey had the drum sticks.

Little Johnny, waving his hand furiously, blurts out, "I know! I know! He's in our bathroom!"

The whole class gets very quiet, looking at the teacher and waiting for his response.

The teacher is completely at a loss for words. He finally gathers his wits and asks Little Johnny how he knows this.

And Little Johnny says, "Well, every morning, my father gets up, bangs on the bathroom door and yells 'Jesus Christ, are you still in there?'"

Family Time

A grandson runs up to his grandfather after Christmas dinner and asks him if he can talk like a frog.

"Of course not," says the grandfather. A few minutes later, his granddaughter goes up to him and asks him the same question.

"No, of course not. Why are you both asking me this?"

The granddaughter replies, "Dad said that when you croak, we can go to Disneyland for Christmas."

Unused Gift

Two friends are talking.

"I've got a problem," says Dave.

"What is it?"

"I'm supposed to buy my wife's mother a present for Christmas. And I'm fresh out of ideas. I mean, it's *her* mother, why can't she buy a gift?"

"What did you buy her last year?" his friend asks.

"Last year I bought her a very expensive cemetery plot."

"Hmmm. It's hard to top that one," says the friend.

The two guys can't come up with any ideas, so Dave doesn't buy his mother-in-law anything for Christmas.

When the big day arrives, the mother-in-law is a bit upset. At dinner, she says out loud to everyone, "Thank you all for the wonderful gifts. Too bad my daughter and son-in-law aren't so thoughtful!"

Suddenly, Dave's six-year-old son says, "Well, you didn't use the gift my dad gave you last year!"

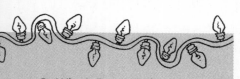

Q: Why is Prancer always wet?

A: Because he's a "rain"-deer.

154

Good Sons

Four brothers leave home for college and become rich, successful doctors and lawyers.

Some years later, the brothers are chatting after having dinner together. They discuss the gifts they bought their elderly mother for Christmas who lives far away in another city.

Q: How can a sleigh possibly fly through the air?

A: If you were being pulled by eight flying reindeer, wouldn't you fly, too?

The first brother says, "I had a big house built for Mama."

The second says, "I had a $100,000 theater built in the house."

The third says, "I bought her a very expensive Mercedes car."

The fourth says, "You know how Mama loves reading the Bible, but she can't read anymore because her vision is bad? Well, I met this preacher who told me about a parrot that can recite the entire Bible! It took 20 preachers 12 years to teach him. I had to contribute $100,000 a year for 20 years to the church, but it was worth it. Mama just has to name the chapter and verse, and the parrot will recite it."

The other brothers are impressed.

After the holidays, their mom sends out a Thank You note to each of her sons:

"Milton, the house you built is so huge. I live in only one room, but I have to clean the whole house. Thanks anyway."

"Marvin, I'm too old to drive. I stay home and have my groceries delivered, so I never use the Mercedes. The thought was good. Thanks."

Q: Where do polar bears vote?

A: The North Poll.

"Michael, you gave me an expensive theater with Dolby sound that can hold 50 people, but all of my friends are dead, I've lost my hearing and I'm nearly blind. I'll never use it. Thank you for the gesture just the same."

"Dearest Melvin, you were the only son to have the good sense to give a little thought to your gift. The chicken was delicious. Thank you."

Mistake

At a high school Christmas party, one young blonde says to another, "Aren't you wearing your boyfriend's promise ring on the wrong finger?"

The other girl replies, "Yes, I am. I promised the wrong boy."

The Perfect Parents

Little Margy's parents are at a Christmas party chatting with some friends when the subject of marriage counseling comes up.

"Oh, we'll never need that. My husband and I have a great relationship," Margy's mom explains. "He took a communications course in college, and I studied theater arts. He communicates really well, and I just act as if I'm listening."

Where Do We Come From?

After a wonderful Christmas Eve sermon at church, a little girl is curious about many things and asks her mother, "How did the human race appear?"

The mother answers, "God made Adam and Eve, and they had children and that was how all people were made."

Two days later, the girl asks her father the same question.

The father answers, "Many, many years ago there were monkeys, and it was from them that the human race evolved."

The confused girl returns to her mother and says, "Mommy, how is it possible that you told me the human race was created by God, and Daddy said they developed from monkeys?"

Q: Why do we hear so many bells at Christmas time?

A: Because so many people ring them.

The mother answers, "Well, dear, it is very simple. I told you about my side of the family, and your father told you about his."

Signs Your Dad Has Had Too Much Christmas Cheer

- You notice the tie sticking out of his fly.

- Someone uses his tongue as a coaster.

- He starts kissing the portraits on the wall.

- His underwear is hanging from the Christmas tree.

- He has to hold onto the floor to keep from sliding off.

- He strikes a match and lights his nose.

- He takes off his socks and wades in the mashed potatoes.

- You hear someone say, "Call a priest!"

- You hear a duck quacking, and it's your dad.

- He complains about the small bathroom after stepping out from the hall closet.

- He refills his glass from the fish bowl.

- He tells everyone he has to go home...and the dinner is at his place.

- He asks for another ice cube and puts it in his pocket.

Signs Your Dad Has Had Too Much Christmas Cheer, continued

- He yawns at the biggest bore in the room...and realizes he's standing in front of the mirror in the hallway.

- He picks up a dinner roll, and butters his watch.

- He suggests everyone stand and sing the national budget.

- He grabs a tissue and blows his ear.

- He's the only one under the coffee table

- He tells his best joke to the rubber plant.

Turkeys for Christmas

A man is driving down a country road one day at 45 miles per hour when suddenly he notices a three-legged turkey running at the same speed beside his truck. Although he thinks this odd, the man decides to speed up so he won't cause an accident with the turkey.

Q: What did Santa say when his toys misbehaved?

A: Toys will be toys.

The man speeds up to 55 miles per hour, but low and behold, so does the three-legged turkey.

Q: What do elves learn in school?

A: The elf-abet

The man then increases his speed to 65 miles per hour, but again the three-legged turkey keeps up to him.

As the man watches in amazement, the turkey suddenly makes a sharp left turn and takes off down a side road toward a small farm.

The man quickly follows the turkey to the farm and parks out front.

Looking around, the man sees a farmer around back standing among hundreds of three-legged turkeys.

After greeting the farmer, the man asks him why he is raising three-legged turkeys.

"Well," says the farmer, "we figure that with an average family of three people, only two of them can have a turkey leg with the average turkey. But with a three-legged turkey, each member of the family can enjoy a turkey leg of their own for Christmas dinner."

"That's pretty wise," says the man, who then asks, "So, what do your three-legged turkeys taste like?"

"I don't know," replies the farmer. "We've never been able to catch one."

CHAPTER NINE

Do You Believe?

Dear Santa, I can explain…

Yes, There Is a Santa Claus

If you want the great gift giver
To come on his sleigh and deliver,
Then remember this simple rhyme
And recall it at Christmas time:
"If in Santa you do not believe,
Christmas gifts you will not receive."

No Worries

Two boys are walking home from Sunday School after hearing a powerful sermon on the devil.

Knock, knock!
Who's there?
Yule!
Yule who?
Yule never know until you open the door!

One boy says, "I'm really scared about all this Satan stuff."

The other boy replies, "Don't worry. You know how Santa Claus turned out…. It's probably just your dad again."

Return to Sender

A four-year-old boy and his father are in the woods looking for a Christmas tree to chop down. They come across a dead bird lying on the snow.

The boy asks his father, "Dad, what happened to the birdie?"

His dad tells him, "Son, the bird died and went to heaven."

The boy replies, "Did God throw him back down?"

Atheist Christmas

An atheist is complaining to his Christian friend. He says, "You Christians have your special holidays, such as Christmas and Easter. Jewish people celebrate their national holidays, such as Passover and Yom Kippur. But we atheists have no recognized national holidays. It's unfair discrimination."

Knock, knock!
Who's there?
Hosanna!
Hosanna who?
Hosanna Claus gets down the chimney I'll never know!

His friend replies, "Why don't you celebrate April first?"

Is He Real?

A few days after Christmas, a six-year-old boy and his mother are talking.

The boy says, "Mom, is there really a Santa Claus?"

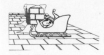

"Well, what do you think?" she asks him.

He replies, "Well, my Xbox that I got and my gift from Santa were wrapped in the same kind of wrapping paper." He thinks for a minute and then says, "But I'll tell you what…you and Dad can still go on buying me presents, and let's just forget we ever had this talk!"

Santa Claus and Coca-Cola

A popular urban myth is that back in 1928, Coca-Cola invented Santa Claus. What started this myth is that his red coat perfectly matches the Coca-Cola colors. The truth is that although early Santa Claus often wore green, Santa Claus in red was established by the 1860s, long before Coca-Cola was invented.

Q: Why does Santa have three gardens?

A: So he can go hoe, hoe, hoe.

Santa Claus' Other Names

Although it is true that the name "Santa Claus" was an American "invention," sometime before 1870, the original name for the "figure" associated with the mid-winter festival was Saint Nicholas, or St. Nick. Other languages have variations or trans-lations of Saint Nicolas, for example, Père Noël, Papa Noel, Babbo Natale, Papai Noel, Father Christ-mas and Kris Kringle.

Dear Lord

A family is having guests for Christmas dinner. At the table, the mother turns to her six-year-old daughter and says, "Dear, would you like to say the blessing?"

"I don't know what to say," shyly replies the little girl.

"Just say what you hear Mommy say, sweetie."

The girl takes a deep breath, bows her head and solemnly says, "Dear Lord, why the hell did I invite all these people to dinner?"

Doubts

A dad figures that his son, at the age of seven, will soon begin to have doubts about Santa Claus. Sure enough, one day the boy announces, "Dad, I know something about Santa Claus, the Easter Bunny and the Tooth Fairy."

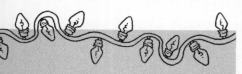

Q: How do you know when Santa's in the room?

A: You can sense his presents.

"Okay, son," says the father. "Let's hear it. What do you know?"

The boy replies with a smile, "They're all nocturnal!"

Modern Christmas

My mom is shopping for Christmas gifts,
With purchases small and large.

164

She doesn't believe in Santa Claus,
She believes in Master Charge!

The Real Santa?

A local newscaster is standing among a crowd of parade watchers who are there to welcome Santa Claus. During a live interview, the reporter asks a bouncy four-year-old girl if she has given her Christmas list to Santa yet.

Knock, knock!
Who's there?
Santa!
Santa who?
Santa Claus!

"No!" she replies.

"Are you going to talk with Santa today?" the newscaster asks.

"No!" she says once again, which was not the response the reporter was expecting at all.

"Why?" he asks the little girl.

"Because the real Santa is at the mall!"

Oops!

Henry knows how to use American Sign Language very well, so he gets hired to be a Santa Claus at the mall. His boss wants to provide hearing-impaired children with a Santa who can communicate with them.

Henry sits in the big leather chair for hours, performing for the children who come to visit Santa. But none of the children that visit him are deaf.

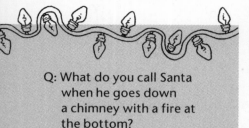

Q: What do you call Santa when he goes down a chimney with a fire at the bottom?

A: Krisp Cringle.

Then, two girls approach him shyly. The older girl explains that her little sister is deaf and cannot speak.

"What is your name?" Henry slowly signs with his fingers.

"J-A-S-M-I-N-E," the little girl replies with her fingers, grinning from ear to ear.

Henry is bubbling over with pride that he can finally use his skills. He is so excited that he accidently signs, "My name is H-E-N-R-Y. Nice to meet you."

Something to Keep In Mind

If you're a worshipper of Satan and you suffer from dyslexia, take care before you commit yourself—you may sell your soul to Santa!

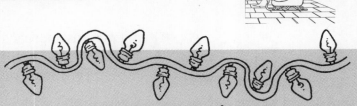

Santa Commandments

- Encourage people to believe in you.

- Always remember who's naughty and who's nice.

- Don't pout.

- It's as much fun to give as it is to receive.

- Some days it's okay to feel a little chubby.

- Make your presents known.

- Always ask for a little bit more than what you really want.

- Bright red can make anyone look good.

- Wear a wide belt and no one will notice how many pounds you've gained.

- If you only show up once a year, everyone will think you're very important.

- Whenever you're at a loss for words, say, "Ho, Ho, Ho!"

CHAPTER TEN

Church Chuckles

*May Christmas be about what's in your heart and
not what's in your pocket!*

Honest Boy

After church service on Christmas Day, a little
boy tells the pastor that he is going to give him
a lot of money when he grows up.

"Well, thank you!" the pastor replies. "That's
very kind of you. But why?"

"Because my daddy says you're one of the poor-
est preachers we've ever had."

A Little Help, Please

One day during Sunday School, the teacher is
telling the kids about how the angel came to Mary
to tell her that she would help bring Jesus into the
world. One little girl
seems puzzled about the
whole story. Then a lit-
tle boy speaks up and
says, "What's the first
thing Mary would have
asked for after the angel
left her?"

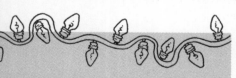

Q: What's red and white and
gives presents to
gazelles?

A: Santelope.

Instantly the little girl says, "I'll bet she asked for a little help from Joseph!"

Good Salesman

Three good little boys look for an after-school job to make money to buy Christmas presents. Their preacher agrees to let them sell Bibles door to door, though he doesn't really want to hire the third boy because he has a speech problem.

Q: What do you give a reindeer with an upset tummy?
A: "Elk"-a-seltzer!

After the first week of work, they all meet at the church. The preacher asks the boys, "How many Bibles did you sell?"

The first boy says, "35."

The second boy says, "75."

The boy with the speech problem says, "I-I-I s-s-sold 175."

The preacher is amazed and asks the boy how he did it.

The boy says, "I-I-I t-t-told them to b-b-buy t-t-them, or I'd r-r-read it to t-t-them."

Mixing Old and New

A little boy returns from Sunday School with a new perspective on the Christmas story. He has learned all about the Wise Men from the East who

Knock, knock!
Who's there?
Snow!
Snow who?
Snow use. I forgot my
name again!

brought gifts to baby Jesus. He is so excited that when he gets home, he says to his parents, "I learned in Sunday School today all about the very first Christmas! There wasn't a Santa Claus way back then, so these three skinny guys on camels had to deliver all the toys! And Rudolph the Red-Nosed Reindeer with his nose so bright wasn't there yet, so they had to have this big spotlight in the sky to find their way around."

Pontius Who?

At a Sunday School in Utah, the younger children are drawing pictures illustrating stories from the Bible. The teacher walks by and notices one little boy is drawing an airplane! "Oh, what Bible story are you drawing?" she asks him.

"This is the Flight into Egypt," the little boy answers. "See, here is Mary, Joseph and baby Jesus. And this," he says, pointing to the front of the plane, "is Pontius. He's the Pilot."

Wise Men

In a small southern town in Georgia, a visitor comes upon a nativity scene in a front yard that shows great skill and talent has gone into creating it. But one small feature bothers the man. The three wise men are wearing firemen's helmets.

Later that day, while at a store on the edge of town, the visitor asks the teenager behind the counter about the helmets. She explodes into a rage, yelling at the man, "You Yankees never do read the Bible!"

The man tells her that he does, but that he simply can't recall anything about firemen in the Bible.

The teenager grabs her Bible from behind the counter and ruffles through some pages. She finally jabs her finger at a passage. Sticking the Bible in the man's face, she says, "See, it says right here, 'The three wise man came from *afar.*'"

Careful!

A young girl is visiting her grandparents to celebrate Christmas. When she walks into their house, the girl sees a beautiful nativity set in the living room.

Q: How do you get into Donner's house?

A: You ring the deer-bell.

The grandmother walks up to her granddaughter and asks her if she knows what it is.

The little girl replies, "Yes…it's breakable."

Christmas Mass

A boy is watching his father, a minister, write a sermon for the Christmas mass.

"How do you know what to say?" asks the boy.

"God tells me," the father answers.

The boy replies, "Oh, then why do you keep crossing things out?"

Prayers Unanswered

A father finds himself in terrible financial trouble. He is so desperate that for the first time in his life, he gets down on his knees and prays to God for help. "Dear God," he prays, "I desperately need your help. I have no money to buy Christmas presents for my family. Could you possibly arrange it so that I win the lottery?"

The lottery draw is held the next day, but the father doesn't win.

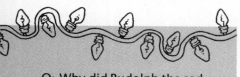

Q: Why did Rudolph the red-nosed reindeer cross the road?

A: Because he was tied to a chicken.

He sends another prayer to God: "My business has gone bust, and if I don't get some money soon, I'll lose my car and my Christmas will be a sad one. Please fix things so I win the next lottery."

Lottery night comes, but the father is unlucky.

So he prays to God again. "Please, God, I'm going to lose my car, and the bank is trying to take my house. Please help me to win the lottery, or my family's Christmas will be ruined."

On lottery night, he again doesn't win anything.

Still hopeful, he prays to God once more. "I am now bankrupt, and the bank took my house and my car. My family is living on the street, but all I need to get my life back together, and perhaps enjoy some kind of Christmas, is to win the lottery."

Suddenly a brilliant flash of light appears as the heavens open, and the man hears the voice of God himself: "Hey, do me a favor will you, and buy a ticket!"

Knock, knock!
Who's there?
Gladys!
Gladys who?
Gladys not me who got coal this Christmas!

Prayer at Christmas

This is how little Johnny prayed at the dinner table on Christmas:

"Dear Jesus, thank you that today's your birthday. I don't know if you have a lot of friends or if you're having a party, but I hope it's your best birthday ever!"

Smart Kid

A teacher asks his class, "Why was Jesus born in Bethlehem?"

A young boy raises his hand and replies, "Because his mother was there."

Church Time

On Christmas Eve, a little girl and her mother go to church. Halfway through the service, the little

Q: Did Rudolph go to a regular school?

A: No, he was "elf"-taught.

girl tells her mother she's going to be sick. Her mother tells her to go in the bushes behind the church. The girl leaves and comes back after about five minutes. Her mother asks her if she threw up.

"Yes," the girl says, smiling. "But I didn't have to go all the way around the back. There was a box near the front door that said 'For the Sick.'"

First Vacation

A Sunday School teacher asks her class why Joseph and Mary took Jesus with them to Jerusalem.

A little girl replies, "They couldn't get a baby-sitter."

Christmas Journey

The Sunday after Christmas, a Sunday School teacher tells her students about an angel appearing to Joseph in a dream, warning him about a danger to the baby Jesus and telling Joseph how to escape from it. After the story time, the teacher tells the students to draw a picture about the story. Most of the pictures are predictable, but Johnny's is different.

"Johnny," says the teacher, "I see that you've drawn a picture of Joseph and Mary with the baby

Jesus on a donkey, but what is that following the donkey?"

"It's the flea, teacher," replies Johnny.

"What flea?" asks the teacher.

To which the boy faithfully repeats the Bible verse: "'Take Mary and Jesus and flee to Egypt.' See, there's Mary, there's Jesus and there's the flea."

Denomination?

Joey's grandmother goes into a post office to buy some stamps for her Christmas cards.

"What denomination do you want?" asks the lady at the counter.

"Good God!" replies the grandmother. "Has it come to this? I suppose you'd better give me 20 Catholic and 20 Presbyterian."

Feed Me

It is a very cold and misty Christmas morning in the very depth of winter after a heavy snowfall, and only one

Q: How does Rudolph know when Christmas is coming?

A: He looks at his calen-"deer"!

farmer and the priest manage to arrive at the church for the morning service.

"Well," says the priest, "I guess there's no point in having a service today."

"That's not how I see it," says the farmer. "If only one cow turns up at feeding time, I still feed it."

Directions, Please

Q: Why do reindeer wear fur coats?

A: Because they look silly in snowsuits.

On the Sunday before Christmas, a priest is walking down the street on his way to visit a friend. However, he needs to mail a present urgently so he asks a young boy on the street where the nearest post office is.

When the boy gives him the directions, the priest thanks him and says, "If you come to church this evening, you will hear me telling everyone how to get to heaven."

The boy replies, "If you don't even know your way to the post office, how will you lead everyone to heaven?"

Army!

Young Jack is coming out of church one day, and the priest standing at the door shakes his hand. The preacher then grabs Jack by the arm and pulls him aside. The priest says to him, "You need to join the Army of the Lord!"

Jack replies, "I'm already in the Army of the Lord."

The priest says, "How come I don't see you in church except at Christmas and Easter?"

Jack whispers "I'm in the secret service."

Help Me, Lord!

On Christmas Day, a little girl is dressed in her nicest church outfit and is running down the street to church so she won't be late.

As she runs, she keeps saying, "Dear God, please don't let me be late for church. Please don't let me be late for church…"

As she is running, she trips and falls.

When she gets back up, she begins praying again, "Please God, don't let me be late for church, but please don't shove me either!"

Quiet!

A mother takes their little boy to church on Christmas Eve.

While in church, the little boy says, "Mommy, I have to pee."

The mother replies, "It's not appropriate to say the word 'pee' in church. So, from now on, whenever you have to pee, just tell me that you have to whisper."

Q: Where do you find reindeer?

A: It depends on where you leave them!

The following Sunday, the little boy goes to church with his father, and during the service, he says to his father, "Daddy, I have to whisper."

The father looks at him and says, "Okay, just whisper in my ear."

CHAPTER ELEVEN

Hanukkah Humor

*To all the people who made me angry, I hope you
get Crocs as a gift.*

Two Friends

Stan and John are walking to school one day,
and Stan is describing his new PlayStation to John.

"Where did you get that?" asks John.

"I got it last night for Hanukkah," says Stan.

"What's Hanukkah?" asks John.

"It's a Jewish holiday, where we get presents
every night for eight nights, to celebrate the festival
of lights."

"Wow, I wish we got that!" John exclaims.

The next day, on the way to school, John runs
up to Stan, curious to see what he got. He notices
that Stan seems to be
upset. "What's wrong?"
asks John. "Where's
your present from last
night?"

Stan holds up a ball of
crumpled wrapping
paper and says, "It was
leftovers night."

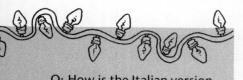

Q: How is the Italian version
of Christmas different?

A: They have one Mary, one
Jesus and 32 wise guys.

Christmas versus Hanukkah

1. Christmas is one day, same day every year: December 25. Jewish people also love December 25. It's another paid day off work. We go to movies, go out for Chinese food and do some Israeli dancing. Hanukkah is eight days. It starts the evening of the 24th of Kislev, whenever that falls. No one is ever sure. Jewish people never know until a non-Jewish friend asks when Hanukkah starts, forcing us to consult a calendar so we don't look like idiots. We all have the same calendar, provided free with a donation from either the World Jewish Congress, the kosher butcher or a Jewish funeral home.

Q: What did the gingerbread man put on his bed?

A: A cookie sheet.

2. Christmas is a major holiday. Hanukkah is a minor holiday with the same theme as most Jewish holidays.

3. Christian kids get wonderful presents such as bikes, board games and iPods. Jewish kids get practical presents such as underwear, socks or the collected works of the Rambam, which looks good on a bookshelf.

4. There is only one way to spell Christmas. No one can decide how to spell Hanukkah: Chanukah, Chanukka, Channukah, Hanukah, Hannukah.

5. Christmas is a time of great pressure for men. Their partners expect special gifts. Jewish men are relieved of that burden. No one expects a diamond ring on Hanukkah.

6. Christmas brings enormous electric bills. Candles are used for Hanukkah. Not only are the electric bills small, but we also get to feel good about not adding to the energy crisis.

8. Christmas carols are beautiful, such as "Silent Night" and "O Come, All Ye Faithful." Hanukkah songs are about dreidels (a four-sided spilling top) made from clay, or we have a party and dance the horah.

9. A home preparing Christmas dinner smells wonderful, with the sweet smell of cookies and cakes baking. Happy people are gathered around in festive moods. A home preparing for Hanukkah smells of oil, potatoes and onions. Both homes, of course, are full of loud people all talking at once.

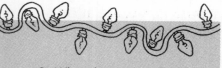

Q: What do you get if you cross a bunny with a white bear?

A: A polar hare.

10. Women have fun baking Christmas cookies. Jewish women burn their eyes and cut their hands grating potatoes and onions for latkes on Hanukkah.

11. Parents give presents to their children during Christmas. Jewish parents have no problem withholding a gift on any of the eight nights.

12. The players in the Christmas story have names that are easy to pronounce, such as Mary, Joseph and Jesus. The players in the Hanukkah story

Q: What do you call a snow-man in the summer?

A: A puddle.

are Antiochus, Judah Maccabee and Matta whatever. No one can spell or pronounce the names. But on the plus side, we can tell our friends anything, and they will believe we know so much about our history.

13. Christmas is becoming more and more about money. The same is true for Hanukkah, even though it is considered a minor holiday. It makes sense. How could we market a major holiday such as Yom Kippur? Forget about celebrating. Think observing. Come to synagogue, starve yourself for 27 hours, beat your chest, confess your sins—a guaranteed good time for you and your family. Tickets are only $200 per person.

Better stick with Hanukkah!

Hanukkah Tree

Admiring the Christmas tree displayed in a neighbor's window, a boy asks his father, "Daddy, can we have a Hanukkah tree?"

"What? No, of course not." says his father.

"Why not?" asks the child.

Surprised, his father replies, "Because the last time we had dealings with a lighted bush we spent 40 years in the wilderness."

Presents!

Just before Hanukkah, a grandmother is giving directions to her grandson who is coming to visit. "You come to the front door of the condominium complex. I'm in apartment 2B."

The grandmother continues, "There's a big panel at the door. With your elbow, push button '2B.' I will buzz you in.

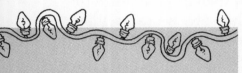

Q: Why are turkeys smarter than chickens?

A: Have you ever heard of Kentucky Fried Turkey?

Come inside. The elevator is on the right. Get in, and with your elbow, hit '2.' When you get out, I am on the left. With your elbow, push my door-bell."

"Grandma, that sounds easy," replies the grandson, "but why am I hitting all these buttons with my elbow?"

The grandmother says, "What? You're coming to visit empty-handed?"

Respect

In a small town in New York, a Catholic priest, a Protestant minister and a Jewish rabbi are very

good friends. Of course, there is a lot of kidding and joking between them all year long.

To their surprise, the priest and the minister receive a Christmas card from the rabbi one year. It reads:

Roses are reddish, violets are bluish

When the Messiah really comes,

You'll wish you were Jewish.

Gifts from Grandma

My grandmother gave me two sweaters for Christmas. One was red, and the other one was blue. The next time my family visited her, I made sure to wear the blue one.

As we entered her home, instead of smiling when she saw me, my grandma said, "Aaron, what's the matter? You didn't like the other sweater?"

Room for the Night

A Jewish lady named Mrs. Rosenberg goes to a fancy hotel, one that does not admit Jewish people. The desk clerk looks down at his book and says, "Sorry, we have no room. The hotel is full."

Knock, knock!
Who's there?
Snow!
Snow who?
Snow business like show business!

Mrs. Rosenberg says, "But your sign outside says that you have vacancies."

183

Q: How many reindeer does it take to change a light bulb?

A: Eight! One to screw in the light bulb and seven to hold Rudolph down!

The desk clerk stutters and then says, "You know that we don't admit Jewish people. Now if you will try the other side of town..."

Mrs. Rosenberg is upset and says, "I'll have you know that I converted to your religion."

The desk clerk says, "Oh, yeah? Okay, let me give you a little test. How was Jesus born?"

Mrs. Rosenberg replies, "He was born to a woman named Mary in a little town called Bethlehem."

"Very good," replies the hotel clerk. "Tell me more."

Mrs. Rosenberg then says, "He was born in a manger."

"That's right," says the hotel clerk. "And why was he born in a manger?"

Mrs. Rosenberg says loudly, "Because a jerk like you in the hotel wouldn't give a Jewish lady a room for the night!"

Why Hanukkah Is Better Than Christmas

1. There's no *Donny and Marie Hanukkah Special* on TV.

2. Eight days of presents (in theory, anyway).

3. No need to clean the chimney.

4. There's no latke-nog.

5. Justin Bieber doesn't sing Hanukkah songs.

6. You won't be pressured to buy Hanukkah Seals.

7. You won't see *You're a Putz, Charlie Brown* on TV.

8. There's no barking dog version of "I Had a Little Dreidel."

9. You don't have pine needles to vacuum up afterwards.

10. Blintzes taste better than old fruitcakes.

Hanukkah at the Deli

During the first day of Hanukkah, two old Jewish grandfathers are sitting in a wonderful deli in New York City. They are talking in Yiddish, the colorful language of Jewish people who came over from Eastern Europe.

185

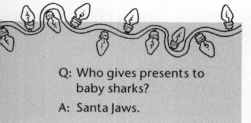

Q: Who gives presents to baby sharks?

A: Santa Jaws.

A Chinese waiter, who has been in the United States for only one year, walks up to them, and in perfect Yiddish, he asks them if everything is okay and if they are enjoying the holiday.

The Jewish men are very surprised. "Where did he learn such perfect Yiddish?" they both think. After they pay the bill, one of the old men asks the deli manager, "Where did your waiter learn such wonderful Yiddish?"

The manager looks around and leans in so no one else will hear and says, "Shhhh. He thinks we're teaching him English."

News Bulletin: Merger of Christmas and Hanukkah

It was announced today that Christmas and Hanukkah will join together for the holidays. It seems the deal has been in the works for about 1300 years.

Although the details were not available at press time, it is believed that the cost of having 12 days of Christmas and eight days of Hanukkah was becoming hard to manage for both sides. By joining the holidays together, the world will be able to enjoy high-quality service during the 15 days of "Chrismukah," as the new holiday is being called.

Huge layoffs are expected, with lords a-leaping and maids a-milking being the hardest hit. As part of the conditions of the agreement, the letters on the dreidel, currently in Hebrew, will be replaced by Latin, meaning that more people won't understand it.

Also, instead of translating to "A great miracle happened there," the message on the dreidel will be "Miraculous stuff happens." In exchange, it is believed that Jewish people will be allowed to use Santa Claus and his large connections for buying and delivering their gifts.

One thing holding up the merger was whether Jewish children could leave milk and cookies for Santa even after they ate meat for dinner. A breakthrough occurred when Oreo cookies were finally declared to be Kosher. Everyone is happy about this.

A spokesman for Santa didn't say whether a takeover of Kwanzaa (an African American type of Christmas celebration) might be in the works as well. Santa then closed the press conference by leading everyone present in a rousing rendition of "Oy Vey, All Ye Faithful."

Q: Why did Frosty have a carrot in his nose?
A: Because he forgot where the refrigerator was.

The Top 10 Reasons Why Everyone Should Celebrate Hanukkah

10. No big, fat guy getting stuck in your chimney.

9. Cleaning wax off your menorah is slightly easier than taking down an eight-foot-tall fir tree.

8. Compare: chocolate gelt versus fruitcake.

7. You get to learn cool new words like "Kislev" and "farshtunken" (stinky).

6. No brutal let-down when you discover that Santa Claus isn't real.

5. Your neighbors won't complain about how your menorah is blinding them senseless.

4. It's like a big reunion when everyone gathers at the Chinese restaurant on Christmas Eve.

3. In a holiday character face-off, Judah Maccabee could kick Frosty's butt.

2. No need to clean up big piles of reindeer poop off your roof.

And the number one reason why everyone should celebrate Hanukkah is:

1. None of that naughty-nice stuff—everyone gets loot!

On a Plane

As a plane settles down at Ben Gurion Airport in Israel, the voice of the pilot comes on: "Please remain seated with your seatbelt fastened until the plane is at a complete standstill

Q: What do snowmen eat for breakfast?
A: Snowflakes.

and the seat belt signs have been turned off.

"To those of you standing in the aisles, we wish you a Happy Hanukkah.

"To those of you remaining in their seats, we wish you a Merry Christmas."

CHAPTER TWELVE

Christmas Miracles

*Christmas light displays are the freestyle rap
battles of the suburbs.*

Fact or Fiction?

- Santa has 31 hours of Christmas to work with,
  thanks to the different time zones and the rota-
  tion of the earth, assuming he travels east to
  west (which seems logical). This works out
  to 822.6 house visits per second. Therefore, for
  each Christian household with good children,
  Santa has 1/1000th of
  a second to park, hop
  out of the sleigh, jump
  down the chimney, fill
  the stockings, put the
  remaining presents
  under the tree, eat
  whatever snacks have
  been left, get back up the chimney, get back
  into the sleigh and move on to the next house.

Q: What do you call Santa
when he stops moving?

A: Santa Pause.

- To reach all these houses, Santa's sleigh would
  have to move at 650 miles per second, which
  is 3000 times the speed of sound. As a com-
  parison, the fastest vehicle on earth, the
  Ulysses space probe, moves at 27.4 miles per

second—a reindeer can run, at the most, 15 miles per hour. So the reindeer need magic or have the some amount of energy as the engines used in *Star Trek*.

- The weight of Santa's sleigh loaded with one Beanie Baby for every kid on earth would be 333,333 tons.

- On land, a reindeer can pull no more than 300 pounds. Even if these "flying reindeer" could pull 10 times the normal amount, 214,200 reindeer would be needed to pull the sleigh.

- That amount of weight traveling at 650 miles per second creates enormous air resistance. The reindeer would heat up in the same way as spacecraft re-entering the earth's atmosphere. The lead pair of reindeer will absorb 14.3 quintillion joules of energy. Per second. Each. In short, they will burst into flame almost instantaneously. The entire reindeer team will be vaporized within 4.26 thousandths of a second.

- In conclusion, if Santa ever did deliver presents on Christmas Eve, he's dead now. Or a different theory is that Santa is magical and is not subject to any of the laws of physics. You just have to believe I guess.

Q: Which side of an Arctic tern has the most feathers?

A: The outside!

Flying Home

A young man is heading home to Chicago to spend Christmas with his parents. When he gets to the airline counter, he presents his ticket, gives the agent his luggage and says, "I'd like you to send my red suitcase to Bermuda and my green suitcase to London."

"I'm sorry, but we can't do that," replies the confused agent.

"Really?" says the young man. "Well, I'm very relieved to hear you say that because that's exactly what you did to my luggage last year!"

Play the Part

A teacher is casting kids for the school's annual Christmas play and is letting her students choose what they want to be, such as Shepherd, Lamb, Villager and so on. One five-year-old boy can't decide what he wants to be, so the teacher says, "Luke, you can be a Villager."

Q: Which elf was the best singer?

A: Elfis Presley.

Luke says, "Okay," and he rushes home to tell his parents. Very excited, he says to them, "Guess what! I get to be a mini-van!"

A Quick Call

In the middle of Christmas dinner, a young girl asks her mother to be excused from the table: "Mom, can I answer the call of nature?" Knowing what her daughter wants, the mom says okay. Immediately, the girl runs to

Q: How many gifts can Santa Claus' bag hold?

A: One less than infinity. Why one less? Because there's a limit to everything.

the bathroom. But, within a minute, she is back.

The mom is shocked by how fast her daughter actually took care of business and asks her how she managed to do it so quickly.

The girl replies, "It was a prank call."

Broken?

Over Thanksgiving weekend, Billy is helping his dad bring the Christmas decorations up from the basement and taking the Halloween and Thanksgiving decorations back down again. During one trek down the stairs with heavy boxes, the dad slips and luckily falls only two steps before landing flat on his behind.

Billy's mom yells from upstairs, "What was that thump?"

"I just fell down the stupid stairs!" says Billy's dad.

"Anything broken?"

"No, I'm fine."

There is just a slight pause before Billy's mom says, "Oh, that's good. What about my decorations? Are any of them broken?"

Working for Your Gift

Danny recently passed his driving test and decides to ask his father, who is a minister, if there is any chance of him getting a car for Christmas, which is still some months away.

Q: What do elves sing to Santa?

A: "Freeze a Jolly Good Fellow!"

"Okay," says his father, "I'll tell you what I'll do. If you can increase your marks in school, study your Bible and get your hair cut, I'll consider the matter very seriously."

A couple of months later, Danny reports back to his father, who says, "I'm really impressed by your commitment to your schoolwork. Your grades are excellent, and the work you have put into your Bible studies is encouraging. However, I have to say, I'm very disappointed that you haven't had your hair cut yet."

Danny is a smart young man who is never lost for an answer. "Look, Dad. During my Bible studies, I've noticed in the illustrations that Moses, John the Baptist, Samson and even Jesus had long hair."

"Yes. I'm aware of that," replies his father. "But did you also notice they walked wherever they went?"

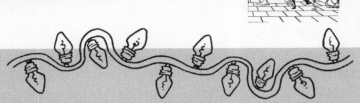

Why Jesus Is Better Than Santa Claus

- Santa Claus lives at the North Pole...
  Jesus is everywhere.

- Santa Claus rides in a sleigh...
  Jesus rides on the wind and walks on the water.

- Santa Claus doesn't know your name—all he can say is, "Hi, little boy (or girl,) what's your name?"
  Jesus not only knows your name, but he also knows how many hairs are on your head.

- Santa Claus has a belly like a bowl full of jelly...
  Jesus has a heart full of love.

- Santa's little helpers make toys...
  Jesus makes new life, mends wounded hearts, repairs broken homes and builds mansions.

- Santa Claus is a "jolly old elf"...
  Jesus is the King of Kings.

Shopping Miracle

A woman is out Christmas shopping with her three young children. After hours of trailing around toy shops and hearing her kids ask for every item on the shelves, she is really fed up. Weighed down with bags, she pushes herself and her kids into a crowded shopping mall elevator and sighs out loud to her fellow shoppers, "Whoever started this whole Christmas thing should be arrested and strung up!"

A small voice in the back replies, "Don't worry—I think they crucified him."

A Walk in the Woods

During Christmas vacation, a city boy visits his cousin who lives on a farm. The two boys are walking through the woods when they see some rabbit turds in the snow. The city boy says, "What are those?"

"They're smart pills," says the other boy. "If you eat them, they'll make you smarter."

So the city boy eats them and then says, "Wow, they taste like crap!"

"See," replies the other boy, "you're getting smarter already."

Wishes

John is on his way with his mother to see Santa Claus at the mall. They are talking about what they want for Christmas.

When John asks his mother what she wants, she says, "Peace and harmony."

John says, "Mom, what's a piece of harmony?"

Q: What goes in a chimney red and comes out of it black?

A: Santa Claus.

Christmas Homework

A young schoolboy is having a hard time pronouncing the letter "W," and all the other kids tease him about it. To help him out, the teacher gives him a sentence to practice at home during Christmas

Q: What eight letters can you find in water from the Arctic Ocean?
A: H to O! (H_2O)

vacation: "William gave Richard a whack on the wrist for wresting the Wheaties from him."

In class after the holidays, the teacher asks the boy to recite the sentence out loud.

The boy nervously looks at his classmates who are already starting to laugh. He swallows hard and then says, "Bill gave Dick a slap on the hand for taking the cereal from him."

Need a Push

It is Christmas Eve. Jim and Shirley have returned from an enjoyable midnight mass at their local church. They arrive home and relax by an open fire before going to bed.

Some time in the middle of the night, they hear a heavy knocking on their front door. Jim goes down stairs and answers the door. In front of him is a young man who is obviously drunk.

"Th'cuse me, thur," the man slurs. "Will you helpth me with a puth?"

Q: What's red, white and blue at Christmas time?

A: A sad candy cane.

"Help you with a push!" says Jim. "You drunken idiot! Get away from my house before I call the police! Irresponsible people like you should be banned from driving!" And he slams the door in the man's face.

Jim goes back to bed and is astonished by what his wife says to him.

"How could you be so mean and uncharitable," she says. "Surely this evening's sermon must still be ringing in your ears. Remember how the innkeeper turned Joseph and Mary away on Christmas Eve? And here you are in the same situation! All that poor man wanted was a push. You are no better than that innkeeper. Shame on you."

Jim is ashamed and full of remorse. He quickly runs down the stairs and opens the front door, but the man is no longer there. Jim runs down the path to his front gate to see if the man or his car are along the road, but there is no traffic or people at all.

On the off-chance that the man might still be around somewhere, he shouts loudly, "Hey, mister needing a push, where are you?!"

The drunken voice replies immediately. "Over here, thur, on the thwing."

Home for the Holidays!

A man in jail wants to escape so he can be with his family in time for Christmas. He decides to dig a hole from his jail cell to the outside world. When finally his work is done, he emerges in the middle of a preschool playground.

"I'm free, I'm free!" he shouts.

"So what," says a little girl standing nearby. "I'm four."

A Little Help, Please!

One Christmas Eve, little Johnny is walking up a big hill pulling his red wagon behind him, saying, "Hell, hell, hell!"

The town priest hears this and walks up to Johnny and says, "You shouldn't swear like that, Johnny. God is all around us at this special time of year."

Q: How much did Santa pay for his sleigh?

A: Nothing; it was on the house.

"Is he in the sky?" asks Johnny.

"Yes," says the priest.

"Is he in that bush over there?" asks Johnny.

"Yes," says the priest.

"Is he in my wagon?" asks Johnny.

"Yes, he is," replies the priest.

"Well, tell him to get the hell out and push!"

Overheard at a School Christmas Party

"Isn't the teacher a bit of a dummy?" says a boy to a girl standing next to him.

"Well, do you know who I am?" asks the girl.

"Umm, no," replies the boy.

"I'm the teacher's daughter," says the girl.

"And do you know who I am?" asks the boy.

"No," she replies.

"Thank goodness!" says the boy before running away.

Now What, My Son?

Pastor Tony is walking down the road on Christmas Eve when he notices Larry, a small boy, trying to press the doorbell of a house across the street. However, Larry is short, and the doorbell is too high for him to reach. After watching the boy's efforts for some time, Tony decides

Q: What is the cleanest reindeer called?

A: Comet.

to help. He walks up behind the little fellow and, placing his hand on the boy's shoulder, leans over and gives the doorbell a solid ring.

Crouching down to Larry's level, Tony smiles kindly and asks, "And now what, my little man?"

Larry replies with a grin, "Now we run!"

Letter to God

George works for the post office after school, and his job is to go through all the mail with unknown addresses. One day a week before Christmas, a letter lands on his desk that is simply addressed "To God."

Q: What's white and red and goes up and down and up and down?

A: Santa Claus in an elevator!

With no other clue on the envelope, George decides to open the letter and reads:

Dear God,

I am a 90-year-old grandmother living alone on a small pension. Yesterday someone stole my purse. It had $100 in it, which was all the money I had in the world. Next week is Christmas, and without that money, I have nothing to buy gifts for my grandchildren. You are my only hope. God, can you please help me?

George is really touched by the letter, and being kind-hearted, he puts a copy of the letter up on the bulletin board for other workers to see. The letter touches everyone at the post office too, and they all dig into their pockets. Between them, they raise $95. Using an official post office envelope, they send the cash to the old lady, and for the rest of the day, all the workers feel a warm glow thinking of the nice thing they have done.

A few days after Christmas, another letter arrives at the post office addressed "To God." Many of the workers gather around while George opens the letter. It reads:

Dear God,

How can I ever thank you enough for what you did for me? Because of your generosity, I was able to buy presents for all my grandchildren. We had a wonderful Christmas, and I told my family about your gift. In fact, we still haven't gotten over it, and even Father John, our priest, is beside himself with joy. By the way, there was $5 missing. I think it must have been one of those thieving workers at the post office.

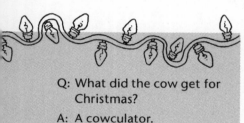

Q: What did the cow get for Christmas?

A: A cowculator.

Christmas Eve Baptism

A curious teenager comes across a baptismal service on Christmas Eve afternoon down by the river in Mississippi.

He decides to walk into the water and stands next to the preacher. The minister says, "Son, are you ready to find Jesus?"

The teenager says, "Yes, preacher, I can do that."

The minister dunks the fellow under the water and pulls him right back up.

"Have you found Jesus?" the preacher asks.

"Nooo, I didn't!" says the teenager.

The preacher then dunks him under the water for quite a bit longer, brings him up, and says, "Now, brother, have you found Jesus?"

"Noooo, I have not," says the man.

The preacher, in disgust, holds the man under for at least 30 seconds this time, brings him out of the water, and says in a harsh tone, "My God, man, have you found Jesus yet?"

The teenager wipes his eyes and says to the preacher, "Are you sure this is where he fell in?"

Candles

While visiting St. Patrick's Cathedral on a tour of New York City during Christmas, a mother and her young son and daughter are awed by the beautiful church.

The kids are especially curious about the candles, so the mother asks if they'd each like to light one, which they do. The mother explains that it is customary to say a prayer of thanks, and she is also careful to tell them that these are not like birthday candles.

"Do you have any questions?" the mother asks.

"No," says the five-year-old girl, "but if there's a pony outside, it's mine."

Knock, knock!
Who's there?
Irish!
Irish who?
Irish you a Merry Christmas!

Humor Cure

A grandfather volunteers to entertain senior citizens in a hospital every year at Christmas time. One year he brings along his young grandson, who takes his portable keyboard.

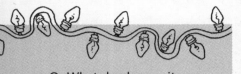

Q: What do elves write on Christmas cards?

A: "Have a fairy happy Christmas."

The grandfather tells some jokes, and the grandson plays his keyboard for the patients.

When the boy is finished, he says, in farewell, "I hope you get better."

One elderly gentleman replies, "I hope you get better, too."

'Twas the Leftovers after Christmas

'Twas the night of Christmas, but I just couldn't sleep.

I tried counting backwards, I tried counting sheep.

The leftovers beckoned, the dark meat and white,

But I fought the temptation with all of my might.

Tossing and turning with anticipation,

The thought of a snack became infatuation!

So I raced to the kitchen,

Flung open the door,

And gazed at the fridge full of goodies galore.

I gobbled up turkey and buttered potatoes,

Pickles and carrots, beans and tomatoes.

I felt myself swelling so plump and so round,

Till all of a sudden, I rose off the ground!

I crashed through the ceiling, floated into the sky

With a mouthful of pudding and a handful of pie.

But I managed to yell

As I soared past the trees,

Happy eating to all,

Pass the cranberries, please!

Please Forgive Me

It is Christmastime, and three very naughty young boys feel guilty for the different bad things they have done. They go to a church to ask for God's forgiveness from the priest.

Q: What vegetable was forbidden on the ships of Arctic explorers?

A: Leeks.

The first boy says to the priest, "Oh, Father! I took my brother's favorite toy and broke it, and now I feel guilty! Please ask God to forgive me!"

The priest gives him a blessing and tells the kid, "God has forgiven you, my son. Now go and drink the water from the well of purity." The priest points at a fountain with sparkling water.

The bad boy goes over to the fountain and drinks the water. "The water tastes weird," he says to himself and walks away.

Q: What do you call a penguin in the Sahara Desert?
A: Lost.

The second naughty boy goes to the priest and says, "Oh, Father! I stole a lot of money from my father's change jar to buy candy, and now I feel guilty. Please ask God to forgive me!"

The priest gives the boy a blessing and says, "God has forgiven you, my son. Now go and drink the water from the well of purity." So the second boy goes to the fountain and takes a drink. "This water tastes funny," he says and goes away.

Now only the third naughty boy remains.

"What did you do wrong, my son?" the priest asks him.

The last kid says, "I peed in the well."

When Santa Got Stuck Up the Chimney

When Santa got stuck up the chimney,
He began to shout,
"You girls and boys
Won't get any toys
If you don't pull me out.
There's soot on my back,
And my beard is all black,
My nose is tickling too."

206

When Santa got stuck up the chimney,
Achoo, Achoo, Achoo!
Was on the eve before Christmas Day,
When Santa Claus arrived on his sleigh.
Into the chimney he climbed with his sack
But he was so fat, he couldn't get back.
Oh, what a terrible plight,
He stayed up there all night.
When Santa got stuck up the chimney,
He began to yell,
"Oh hurry, please,
It's all such a squeeze,
The reindeer's stuck as well!"
His head's up there in the cold night air,
Now Rudolph's nose is blue!
When Santa got stuck up the chimney,
Achoo, Achoo, Achoo, Achoo, Achoo, Achoo,
Achoo!

An Australian Christmas

Here comes Santa Claus, here comes Santa
Claus,
Sweating his fat away.
Here comes Santa Claus, here comes Santa
Claus,
Water-skis on his sleigh.

Never have a white Christmas.

Q: What's another name for ice?
A: Skid stuff!

When in Melbourne you live.
Wearing hot pants on the beach
When you your presents give.

Here comes Santa Claus, here comes Santa Claus,
Sweating his fat away.
Here comes Santa Claus, here comes Santa Claus,
Water-skis on his sleigh.

Chestnuts roasting on the sidewalk.
Castles in the sand,
Eating ice cream, having good talks,
Warm Christmas, isn't that grand?

CHAPTER THIRTEEN

Christmas Quizzes, Facts and Funny Flubs

The nice thing about Christmas is that you can make people forget the past with a present.

Ruining Christmas Song Lines

No one can flub a Christmas carol better than a kid. Sing along with these new takes on old favorites (the real lyrics are included):

- Deck the halls with Buddy Holly (Deck the halls with boughs of holly)
- We three kings of porridge and tar (We three kings of Orient are)
- On the first day of Christmas, my tulip gave to me (On the first day of Christmas, my true love gave to me)

Q: Who sings "Blue Christmas" and makes toy guitars?

A: Elfis.

- Later on we'll perspire, as we dream by the fire (Later on we'll conspire, as we dream by the fire)
- He's making a list, chicken and rice (He's making a list and checking it twice)

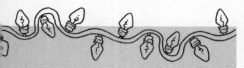

Q: What sits on the bottom of the cold Arctic Ocean and shakes?

A: A nervous wreck.

• Noel, Noel, Barney's the king of Israel (Noel, Noel, Born is the King of Israel)

• Olive, the other reindeer (All of the other reindeer)

• Frosty the snowman is a ferret elf, I say (Frosty the snowman is a fairy tale they say)

• Sleep in heavenly peas (Sleep in heavenly peace)

• In the meadow we can build a snowman, then pretend he's sparse and brown (In the meadow we can build a snowman, then pretend that he is Parson Brown)

• You'll go down in Listerine (You'll go down in history)

• Oh, what fun it is to ride with one horse, soap and hay (On, what fun it is to ride on a one-horse open sleigh)

• Come, froggy faithful (O Come, All Ye Faithful)

• Good tidings we bring to you and your kid (Good tidings we bring to you and your kin)

Christmas Around the World

Here's how to say "Merry Christmas!" in other languages. Try them out on your friends.

- Afrikaans: Geseënde Kersfees
- Afrikander: Een Plesierige Kerfees
- Albanian: Gezur Krislinjden
- Brazilian: Feliz Natal
- Chile and Spanish: Feliz Navidad
- Chinese: (Cantonese) Gun Tso Sun Tan'Gung Haw Sun
- Chinese: (Mandarin) Sheng Dan Kuai Le Choctaw: Yukpa, Nitak Hollo Chito
- Cree: Mitho Makosi Kesikansi
- Czech: Prejeme Vam Vesele Vanoce a stastny Novy Rok
- Dutch: Vrolijk Kerstfeest en een Gelukkig Nieuwjaar or Zalig Kerstfeast
- English: Merry Christmas (of course!)
- Finnish: Hyvaa joulua
- French: Joyeux Noel
- German: Fröhliche Weihnachten
- Greek: Kala Christouyenna!
- Hungarian: Boldog Karácsonyt
- Indonesian: Selamat Hari Natal

Christmas Around the World, continued

- Irish: Nollaig Shona Dhuit or Nodlaig Mhaith Chugnat
- Italian: Buone Feste Natalizie
- Japanese: Shinnen omedeto. Kurisumasu Omedeto
- Korean: Sung Tan Chuk Ha
- Latin: Natale hilare et Annum Faustum
- Navajo: Merry Keshmish
- Norwegian: God Jul or Gledelig Jul
- Philippines: Maligayang Pasko
- Polish: Wesolych Swiat Bozego Narodzenia or Boze Narodzenie
- Russian: Pozdrevlyayu s prazdnikom Rozhdestva is Novim Godom
- Swedish: God Jul and (Och) Ett Gott Nytt År
- Thai: Sawadee Pee Mai or souksan wan Christmas
- Ukrainian: Z Rizdvom Khrystovym or S Rozhdestvom Kristovym
- Vietnamese: Chuc Mung Giang Sinh

Christmas Facts

- Many people in European countries believed that spirits, both good and evil, were active during the 12 days of Christmas. These spirits eventually evolved into Santa's elves, especially under the influence of the book *The Night Before Christmas*, which was written by Clement C.

Moore (1779–1863) and illustrated by Thomas Nast (1840–1902).

- Each year, there are approximately 20,000 "Rent-a-Santas" across the United States. Rent-a-Santas usually take seasonal training on how to maintain a jolly attitude under pressure from the public. They also receive practical advice, such as not accepting money from parents while children are looking, and they should not eat garlic, onions or beans for lunch.

Q: What's the most popular Christmas wine?

A: I don't like Brussels sprouts!

- Evergreen (from the Old English words *aefie* meaning "always" and *gowan* meaning "to grow") trees have been symbols of eternal life and rebirth since ancient times. The pagan use and worship of evergreen boughs and trees has evolved into the Christianized Christmas tree.

- It is believed that Christmas stockings evolved from three sisters who were too poor to afford a marriage dowry and were, therefore, doomed to a life of poverty. The sisters were saved, however, when the wealthy Bishop Saint Nicholas of Smyrna (the precursor to Santa Claus) crept down their chimney and generously filled their stockings with gold coins.

- The earliest known Christmas tree decorations were apples. At Christmas time, medieval actors would use apples to decorate "paradise" trees (usually fir trees) during "Paradise Plays," which were plays depicting Adam and Eve's creation and fall.

Favorite Team

On the first day of school after the Christmas break, a teacher asks her class, "Who here is a Maple Leafs fan?"

Every student knows she loves the Leafs, so they reply by raising their hands, except for one boy named Todd.

The teacher asks, "Who do you like, Todd?"

Todd replies, "I'm a Montreal Canadiens fan, and I hate the Leafs."

The teacher asks why, and Todd tells her that his dad is a fan of the Habs, so he is, too.

The teacher says to the rest of the class, "So if Todd's father was an idiot, what would that make Todd?"

Todd quickly says, "A Leafs fan!"

Got a Room?

Did you hear about the Christmas pageant at a school in Beverly Hills? Two kids dressed as Mary and Joseph, and they are on their way to the inn in Bethlehem. On the other side of the stage, a boy in a shepherd's outfit is on a cellphone—he was calling for reservations.

Christmas Tongue Twister Story

(Read out loud—it helps!)

This is a stairy fory.

Tonce upon a wime there was a gritty little pearl named Prinderella. She lived with her two sisty uglers and her nicked wepstother. She weaned the clindows,

Q: What's an ig?
A: A snow house without a loo!

flubbed the scores and did all the wirty durk, which was a shirty dame.

Don way the Cince issued a cropplamation that all geligable lung yadies should attend a drancy fess bistmas crawl.

Now poor Prinderella didn't have a drancy fess; all she had was a rirty dag.

Then, along came her gairy fedmother and in the eyeling of a twink she turned her rirty dag into a drancy fess.

So, Prinderella bent to the wall and pranced and pranced with the Cince. But, on the moke of stridnight she ran down the stalace peps and on the stottom bep slopped a dripper; which was, of course, another shirty dame.

The dext nay, the Cince issued another croplamation that all geligable lung yadies who had

Q: Why is the slippery ice like music?

A: If you don't C sharp, you'll B flat!

attended the drancy fess ball, should sly on the tripper.

When the sisty uglers slied on the tripper, it fiddent dit. But when Prinderella slied on the tripper it fid dit.

So, the moo were tarried and mived yappily afty everward.

Brain Twister

Read each line without making any mistakes. If you make a mistake, you *must* start over or it won't work.

This is this Santa

This is is Santa

This is how Santa

This is to Santa

This is keep Santa

This is a Santa

This is dummy Santa

This is busy Santa

This is for Santa

This is forty Santa

This is seconds Santa

Now go back and read the third word in each line from the top. Betcha can't resist passing it on.

Funny Quotes About Christmas Stuff

Today, President Obama announced that he's giving all federal employees Christmas Eve off. And when Joe Biden heard that he was like, "But not Santa, right?"

—Jimmy Fallon, TV host of Late Night
with Jimmy Fallon

I bought my brother some gift wrap for Christmas. I took it to the gift wrap department and told them to wrap it, but in a different print so he would know when to stop unwrapping.

—Steven Wright, comedian

My grandmother, she passed away at Christmas time. So now, I have this built in sadness, you know, every holiday. 'Cause I'm plagued with the thought of, you know, what she would have given me. What didn't I get to open this year?

—Laura Kightlinger, actress/comedian

There is a remarkable breakdown of taste and intelligence at Christmastime. Mature, responsible grown men wear neckties made of holly leaves and drink alcoholic beverages with raw egg yolks and cottage cheese in them.

—P.J. O'Rourke, humorist

Q: How do you keep from getting cold feet?

A: Don't go around BRRfooted!

This past Christmas, I told my girlfriend for months in advance that all I wanted was an Xbox. That's it. Beginning and end of list, Xbox. You know what she got me? A homemade frame with a picture of us from our first date together. Which was fine. Because I got her an Xbox.

—*Anthony Jeselnik, stand-up comedian*

I once bought my kids a set of batteries for Christmas with a note on it saying, "Toys not included."

—*Bernard Manning, comedian*

I stopped believing in Santa Claus when I was six. Mother took me to see him in a department store, and he asked for my autograph.

—*Shirley Temple, child actor*

Aren't we forgetting the true meaning of Christmas? You know...the birth of Santa.

—*Bart Simpson, cartoon character*

More Funny Quotes About Christmas

- All I want for Christmas is youuuuuuuu…to get hit by a reindeer.

- My boyfriend is just like Santa Claus. He gives me presents and is imaginary.

- Last Christmas I gave you my heart, but the very next day, your body rejected the transplant and you died.

- A song told me to Deck the Halls, so I did. Mr. and Mrs. Hall are not very happy.

- My neighbor put up his Christmas lights today. I bet he's mad that I beat him to it. I put mine up three years ago.

- I try to be unusually kind and compassionate to those around me during the holidays, because I never know who will end up being my Secret Santa.

News Bulletin: True Christmas Story

A seven-year-old boy was stopped by police in Germany while trying to plow snow with a front loader he borrowed from his parents' business. Police officers on patrol found the boy sitting in a snow plow after he had cleared the street in the town of Reinfeld and was driving

Q: What did the ocean say to the bergy bits?

A: Nothing. It just waved. (That's an old joke from the Ice Age.)

Q: Why aren't penguins as lucky as arctic murres?

A: The poor old penguins can't go south for the winter.

back to the parking lot. The child noticed the police car behind him and stopped immediately.

The boy opened the door, got out and admitted immediately that he did not have a driver's license. When the police asked the boy why he was plowing, he said his father had complained that the roads were awful at Christmastime. The boy saw the key in the ignition of the vehicle and set off.

Gift Buying

Sarah: "I wanted to buy my grandmother a packet of handkerchiefs for her Christmas stocking, but I've changed my mind."

Mary: "Why did you change your mind?"

Sarah: "I don't know what size her nose is!"

Stupid People at Christmas!

Here are some weird facts from Canada that will make you want to be careful at Christmas:

1. Hospitals reported four broken arms last year after cracker-pulling accidents.
2. Three people die each year testing if a nine-volt battery works on their tongue.
3. Five people were injured last year in accidents involving out-of-control electric cars.

4. Eight people cracked their skull after falling asleep while throwing up into the toilet.

5. Eighteen people had serious burns trying on a new sweater with a lit cigarette in their mouth.

6. Nineteen people have died in the last three years believing that Christmas decorations were chocolate.

7. Thirty-one people died by watering their Christmas tree while the lights were plugged in.

8. Fifty-eight people are injured each year by using sharp knives instead of screwdrivers.

9. One hundred people had broken parts of plastic toys pulled out of the soles of their feet.

10. One hundred and forty people were injured by not removing all the pins from new shirts.

11. More than 500 people were admitted to hospital in the last two years after opening bottles of beer with their teeth.

How Poor?

Suzie: "My family had a very poor Christmas this year."

Carla: "Oh, that's too bad. Why was it poor?"

Suzie: "We couldn't afford tinsel. We had to wait for grandpa to sneeze."

Q: What's the difference between a walrus and a banana?

A: You'd better find out before you ever try to peel a walrus.

Say It Slowly

My Uncle Brian was visiting us at Christmas last year, and he said to my dad, "Man, my son is flunking the third grade. I don't know how to tell my kid he's probably going to be held back a year."

My dad replied, "Well, I guess you better tell him slowly so the little dummy will get it."

Pleeeeeeease!

Little Joe: "Mom, can I please have a cat for Christmas?"

Mom: "No. You'll have turkey just the same us the rest of us."

A Christmas Baby!

Michael is very excited that his mom is going to have a Christmas baby. When the time comes, Michael's dad gets very nervous and frantically calls the doctor. He yells into the phone, "My wife is ready to have a baby and her contractions are only two minutes apart!"

"Is this her first child?" the doctor asks.

"No, you idiot!" the man shouts. "This is her husband!"

Q: What do chefs in Alaska call "Baked Alaska"?

A: "Baked Here."

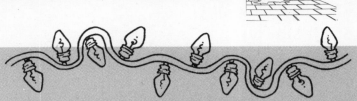

Christmas Fun Facts

- There are currently 78 people named "S. Claus" living in the United States—and one "Kriss Kringle." (You gotta wonder about that kid's parents.)

- December is the most popular month for nose jobs.

- The average wage of a mall Santa Claus: $11 an hour. With real beard: $20.

- No species of reindeer can fly. However, there are 300,000 species of living organisms yet to be classified, and while most of these are insects and germs, this does not completely rule out flying reindeer, which only Santa has ever seen.

- The common abbreviation for "Christmas" to "Xmas" is derived from the Greek alphabet. "X" stands for "Chi," which is the first letter of Christ's name in the Greek alphabet.

- Mexicans call the poinsettia the "Flower of the Holy Night"—the Holy Night is the Mexican way of saying "Christmas Eve."

- Robert L. Ripley (founder of Ripley's Believe It Or Not!) and NBA star Eric Gordon were both born on Christmas Day.

- On Christmas tree decorations, angels are usually shown as wimpy blondes in fluffy blouses and sandals. In the Bible, however, angels are muscular bullies who often challenge humans into fistfights.

- The world's largest Christmas present was the Statue of Liberty. The French gave it to the U.S. in 1886. It is 150 feet high and weights 225 tons! ☞

Christmas Fun Facts, continued

- It can take up to 15 years to grow an average-sized tree of 6–7 feet or as little as four years, but the average growing time is seven years!

- According to the Guinness World Records, the tallest Christmas tree ever cut was a 221-foot Douglas fir that was displayed in 1950 at the Northgate Shopping Center in Seattle, Washington.

- Norwegian scientists believe that Rudolph's red nose is probably the result of a parasitic infection of his respiratory system.

- All the gifts in the "Twelve Days of Christmas" would equal 364 gifts. That's a whole lot of wrapping paper!

- In Poland, spiders or spider webs are common Christmas trees decorations because according to legend, a spider wove a blanket for baby Jesus. In fact, Polish people consider spiders to be symbols of goodness and prosperity at Christmas. Who knew!

- For many people in Japan, a trip to Kentucky Fried Chicken (KFC) is a must on Christmas Day. The line-ups are sometimes so long that people phone to make reservations. Finger lickin' good!

- Mistletoe is often call the "poop twig"! A bird will eat a mistletoe berry and then fly away. Later, as the bird is flying in the sky, it will poop, and the poop lands in the tree. When the mistletoe first sprouts, it looks like a twig. The word "mistletoe" comes from the Anglo-Saxon word misteltan ("mistel" means poop, and "tan" means twig). Mistletoe is therefore a poop twig!

Poor Puppy

On returning to school after the holidays, Johnny's teacher asks the class how their Christmas vacation was. Johnny is the first to speak.

"My Christmas vacation was horrible," says Johnny. "A car hit my new dog in the bum!"

"Rectum!" says the teacher. "Say 'rectum.'"

"Rectum?" replies Johnny. "Damn near killed 'em!"

ABCs

It is a week before the kindergarten Christmas concert, and little Wilfred is practicing his ABCs, but he is very scared of saying them in front of a big audience at school. The teacher, though, tells him that the best way to conquer his fears is to practice and to just go ahead and do it. So, trembling, Wilfred stands in front of the class and begins.

Q: What kind of math do Snowy Owls like?
A: Owlgebra.

"ABCDEFGHIJLKMNOQRSTUVWXYZ."

"Very good, Wilfred," says the teacher, "but you forgot the 'P.' Where's the 'P'?"

"It's running down my leg."

Excuses, Excuses

These are excuse notes from "parents" to explain their child's absence from the Christmas school concert:

- My son is under a doctor's care and should not be in the concert. Please execute him.
- Please excuse Lisa for being absent. She was sick and I had her shot.
- Dear School: Please excuse John being absent on December 28, 29, 30, 31, 32 and also 33.
- Please excuse Roland from the concert. Yesterday he fell off the roof while shoveling snow and misplaced his hip.
- John can't be in the concert because he had two teeth taken out of his face.
- Megan cannot be in the concert because she has been bothered by very close veins.
- Chris will absent cuz he has an acre in his side.
- Please excuse Ray from the concert. He has very loose vowels.
- Irving was absent because he missed his bust.
- Please excuse Jimmy for not being there. It was his father's fault.
- I kept Martha home because she had to go Christmas shopping because I don't know what size she wears.
- Sally won't be in the concert. We have to attend her funeral.
- Please excuse Jason for being absent. He had a very bad cold and could not breed well.

Fascinate Me!

After Christmas vacation, a teacher asks her students to make up a sentence with the word "fascinate" and "Christmas" in it. A little girl says, "Christmas Day was fascinating."

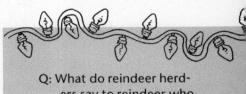

Q: What do reindeer herders say to reindeer who complain?

A: "Venison!"

The teacher says, "No, I said use 'fascinate.'"

Another little girl says, "There was so much fascination to see at Christmas time."

The teacher again says, "No, use the word 'fascinate.'"

Little Johnny yells from the back of the room, "My mom ate so much turkey on Christmas Day that she could only fasten eight of the 10 buttons on her shirt!"

Kid Wisdom at Christmas Time

- Never trust a dog to watch your food. –Patrick, 10
- When your dad is mad and asks you, "Do I look stupid?" don't answer him. –Michael, 14
- Never tell your mom her diet's not working. –David, 12
- Stay away from fruitcake. –Randy, 9
- Puppies have bad breath, even after eating a Tic Tac. –Andrew, 9

- Never hold a dust buster and your new kitten at the same time. –Karen, 9
- You can't hide a piece of broccoli in a glass of milk. –Armir, 9
- If you want a cat for Christmas, start out by asking for a horse. –Naomi, 14
- Your new felt markers are not good to use as lipstick. –Lauren, 9
- Don't pick on your sister when she's holding a baseball bat. –Joel, 10
- Never try to baptize your new kitten. –Eileen, 8

Bored During Vacation

A retired man moves near a junior high school. He spends the first few months in peace and quiet, but during the Christmas holidays, three young boys beat on every trashcan in the neighborhood because they are bored.

Finally, the man can't take the noise any longer so he decides to take action and goes out to talk to the boys. He says, "You kids are a lot of fun. I'll give you each a dollar if you promise to come around every day during your vacation and do your thing."

The boys agree and continue to do a bang-up job on the trashcans.

After a few days of the boys hitting the trash-cans, the man tells them, "This recession is really putting a big dent in my income. From now on, I'll only be able to pay you 50 cents to beat on the cans."

The noisemakers aren't happy about this, but they accept the old man's offer anyway.

Two days later, the man approaches them again. "Look," he says, "I haven't received my pension check yet, so I'm not going to be able to pay you more than 25 cents. Will that be okay?"

"A freakin' quarter?!" the drum leader exclaims. "If you think we're going to waste our holidays beating these cans around for just a quarter, you're nuts. We quit!"

At a Christmas Wedding

A little boy is in a relative's wedding during Christmas. As he is walking down the aisle, he takes two steps, stops and turns to the crowd (alternating between the bride's side and groom's side). While facing the crowd, he puts his hands up like claws and roars. So it goes—step, step, "roar," step, step, "roar," all the way down the aisle. The people in the church are laughing very hard by the time the boy reaches the altar.

The little boy, however, is getting more and more distressed from all the laughing, and he is almost ready to cry.

When the bride asks the boy what he was doing, he sniffs and says, "I was being the Ring Bear."

Christmas Excitement

A young boy is excited about Christmas and can't fall asleep after his father sends him to bed. Five minutes later, the boy screams, "Dad! Can you get me a glass of water?"

The dad says, "No. You had your chance before you went to bed."

A minute later the boy screams, "Dad! Can you get me a glass of water, please?"

The dad says, "No. You had your chance. Next time you ask, I'll come up there and spank you."

"Dad," the little boy replies, "when you come up to spank me, can you bring me a glass of water?"

More Excited Kids

It's the last day of school before Christmas vacation and all the kids can't wait for the class to end. In one science class, a teacher asks a student a question, but she can barely hear the child speak since the other students are making too much noise. In an attempt to quiet them, she says loudly, "I can hear voices!"

Q: What's Santa's favorite candy?

A: Jolly Ranchers.

Two janitors sweeping the hallway outside the classroom hear the teacher, and one says to the other, "Geez, she better stop telling the kids about her mental problems!"

At the Movies

During Christmas vacation, two young girls go to the mall to watch their first movie. They each buy one ticket and go in.

Q: What did the detective in the Arctic say to the robbery suspect?

A: "Where were you on the night of September to March?"

A minute later, one of the girls comes back out to buy another ticket. The man at the counter asks, "Why do you want another one?"

The girl replies, "Because that man over there ripped the first one in half."

Shut-up and Trouble

In a small town in California lives two boys, Shut-up and Trouble. The boys are friends, but every once in a while they get into a fight. One day at the mall during their Christmas vacation, they both buy an ice cream cone, but Trouble's ice cream falls to the floor. Trouble then steals Shut-up's ice cream and runs away. Shut-up chases after Trouble but eventually loses him when he runs down the escalator, so Shut-up sits on the nearest bench and starts to cry.

A security officer spots him and says, "What's your name?"

"Shut-up."

Q: What's the difference between an iceberg and a clothes brush?

A: One crushes boats, and the other brushes coats.

The officer gets angry and asks the same question again and gets the same reply. After he asks the question again and gets the same answer, he says, "Boy, are you looking for trouble?"

And Shut-up says, "Yeah, that fool stole my ice cream!"

Stand Up!

A school hires a substitute teacher right before Christmas. The new teacher tries to make use of the psychology courses she has taken. The first day of class, she says to the class, "Everyone who thinks they're stupid, stand up!"

After a few seconds, Little Johnny stands up.

The teacher asks, "Do you think you're stupid, Johnny?"

"No, ma'am, but I hate to see you standing there all by yourself."

Visiting Grandpa

A young city girl is visiting her grandfather's farm in California at Christmas, and she notices a wheelbarrow full of cow manure by the side of the house. The girl asks her grandpa what he is going to do with all that cow poop.

The farmer says, "I'm going to it put on my strawberries."

The little girl looks up at her grandfather and says, "I don't know about you, but where I come from, we put cream and sugar on our strawberries."

A Christmas Quiz

In each sentence below, fill in the blanks with an expression commonly used at Christmas time. Answers are at the end of page 235.

1. On December 24, Adam's wife was known as

   _____ .

2. In Charles Dickens's *A Christmas Carol*, Scrooge was visited by the ghost of _____ .

3. An opinion survey in Alaska could be called a _____ .

4. When salt and pepper say "Hi!" to each other, they are passing on _____ .

5. An old man without coins could be called

   _____ .

6. When you cross a sheep with a cicada, you get a _____ .

7. A medieval armor-wearer who is quiet is called a _____ .

8. A cat walking on the desert is bound to get

   _____ .

9. Actor O'Connor and actress Channing are known on December 25 as _____ .

10. People who tell jokes on December 25 might be called _____ .

Here's Another Christmas Quiz!

The answers are on page 235.

1. What's the name of the period leading up to Christmas?

2. How many Wise Men brought gifts to Jesus?

3. Who brings presents to children in Holland on December 6?

4. In what town was Jesus born?

5. In what decade was the first Christmas card sent in the United Kingdom?

6. How many of Rudolph's eight companions' names start with the letter 'D'?

7. In what country did Christmas trees originate?

8. What's the second line of the song "I'm Dreaming of a White Christmas"?

9. What was Joseph's job?

10. Who started the custom of Wassailing (a way to pass on good wishes to family and friends)?

11. Who were the first people to visit the baby Jesus?

12. What item is considered lucky to find in your Christmas pudding in Britain?

13. What angel visited Mary?

14. Where did the baby Jesus sleep?

Answers to "A Christmas Quiz"

1. Christmas Eve
2. Christmas Present
3. North Poll
4. Season's greetings
5. St. Nickleless
6. Bah! (or Baa!) Humbug!
7. Silent knight
8. Sandy claws
9. Christmas Carols
10. Christmas cards

Answers to "Here's Another Christmas Quiz!"

1. Advent
2. More than one—the Bible doesn't say how many
3. St. Nicholas
4. Bethlehem
5. 1840s (1843 by Sir Henry Cole)
6. Three (Dasher, Dancer and Donner)
7. Germany (It was Latvia, but it was part of Germany then.)
8. "Just like the ones I used to know"
9. Carpenter
10. The Anglo Saxons—it means "good health"
11. Shepherds
12. A sixpence
13. Gabriel
14. In a manger

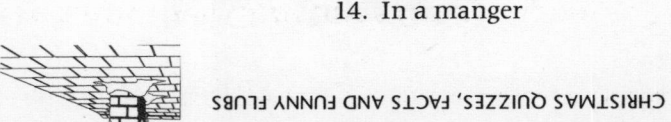

CHAPTER FOURTEEN

More Riddles

Q: What do Arctic hares use to keep their fur looking spiffy?
A: Hare spray.

Q: Why are bad school grades like a shipwreck in the Arctic Ocean?
A: They're both below C level.

Q: What are caribou babies given to wear?
A: Hoof-me-downs.

Q: Why does Santa's sled get such good mileage?
A: Because it has long-distance runners on each side.

Q: Which reindeer have the shortest legs?
A: The smallest ones.

Q: Who lives at the North Pole, makes toys and rides around in a pumpkin?
A: Cinder-elf-a.

Q: If athletes get athlete's foot, then what do astronauts get?
A: Missile-toe.

Q: What do angry mice send to each other at Christmas?
A: Cross-mouse cards.

Q: How do you scare a snowman?
A: Show him your hairdryer.

Q: How do you know if there's a snowman in your bed?
A: You wake up wet!

Q: What do you get when you cross a cat with Santa Claus?
A: Santa Claws.

Q: What did the ghost say to Santa Claus?
A: I'll have a boo Christmas without you.

Q: Where do seals go to see movies?
A: The dive-in!

Q: What's red and white, red and white, red and white?
A: Santa Claus rolling down a hill.

Q: What's black and white and red all over?
A: Santa covered with chimney soot.

Q: Why is Santa so good at karate?
A: Because he has a black belt.

Q: If the sun shines while it's snowing, what should you
   look for?
A: Snowbows.

Q: What did one Greenland shark say to the other?
A: "Say, good lookin', didn't I meet you last night at the
   feeding frenzy?"

Q: Santa rides in a sleigh. What do elves ride in?
A: A mini-van.

Q: Where do you find elves?
A: Depends where you left them.

Q: Why do mummies like Christmas so much?
A: Because of all the wrapping.

Q: What did the elf say was the first step in using a Christmas computer?
A: "First, Yule Log on."

Q: Where can you find an ocean without any water?
A: On a map.

Q: What do the Ninja turtles do on Christmas?
A: They shellabrate.

Q: What did one Arctic murre say to the other?
A: "What? We flew 2000 miles for this?!"

Q: What do elves use to go from floor to floor?
A: An elf-evator.

Q: What comes before Christmas Eve?
A: Christmas Adam!

Q: How do elves greet each other?
A: "Small world, isn't it?"

Q: What is the favorite food of elves?
A: Elf-aghetti.

Q: What nerve is used to sense elves?
A: The elfactory nerve.

Q: How long should a reindeer's legs be?
A: Just long enough to reach the ground.

Q: What did the Christmas tree say to the ornament?
A: Aren't you tired of hanging around?

Q: How many elves does it take to change a light bulb?
A: Ten. One to change the light bulb, and nine to stand on each other's shoulders.

Q: Why did SpongeBob have a great Christmas?
A: Because he kissed a Krabby Patty.

Q: What do you use to catch an Arctic hare?
A: A hare net.

Q: What did the Christmas tree say to the ornament?
A: Aren't you tired of hanging around?

ABOUT THE AUTHOR

DAVID MACLENNAN is a writer and photographer. He earned his BA in English literature from McGill University and his graduate diploma in journalism from Concordia University. He has been collecting jokes of various genres for some time and has written seven other joke books.

ABOUT THE ILLUSTRATORS

PETER TYLER is a graduate of the Vancouver Film School's Visual Art and Design and Classical animation programs. Though his ultimate passion is in filmmaking, he is also intent on developing his draftsmanship and storytelling, with the aim of using those skills in future filmic misadventures.

ROGER GARCIA is a self-taught freelance illustrator based out of Alberta who works in acrylics, ink and digital media. His illustrations have been published in humor books, children's books, newspapers and educational material.

When Roger is not at home drawing, he can be seen facilitating cartooning workshops at various elementary schools, camps and local art events. Roger also enjoys participating with colleagues in art shows, painting murals in schools and public places.